The Meditative Mind

A Selection of Passages
from the Teachings of
J. Krishnamurti

STUDY BOOK SERIES

A series of Study Books was conceived for use as concentrated study material on a particular topic. These books are an invaluable resource of excerpted material as they offer a sustained survey of each topic, allowing for a deeper comprehension of what Krishnamurti was conveying. Much of the material has been drawn from his works and the record of his public talks from 1933 to 1967. The following books have been published :

- **Action**
  [ISBN : 978-81-208-3273-2]
- **The Meditative Mind**
  [ISBN : 978-81-208-3272-5]
- **The Mirror of Relationship : Love, Sex and Chastity**
  [ISBN : 978-81-208-3274-9]
- **Individual & Society : The Bondage of Conditioning**
  [ISBN : 978-81-208-3275-6]
- **The Observer and the Observed**
  [ISBN : 978-81-208-3276-3]

Study Book Series

The Meditative Mind

A Selection of Passages
from the Teachings of
J. Krishnamurti

MOTILAL BANARSIDASS PUBLISHERS
PRIVATE LIMITED • DELHI

First Indian Edition : Delhi, 2012
First Published : USA, 1989

In Association With
KRISHNAMURTI FOUNDATION OF AMERICA
P.O. Box 1560, Ojai, California 93024 U.S.A
E-mail: kfa@kfa.org.Website: www.kfa.org

ISBN : 978-81-208-3272-5

Editor : WM. D. QUINN

MOTILAL BANARSIDASS
41 U.A. Bungalow Road, Jawahar Nagar, Delhi 110 007
8 Mahalaxmi Chamber, 22 Bhulabhai Desai Road, Mumbai 400 026
203 Royapettah High Road, Mylapore, Chennai 600 004
236, 9th Main III Block, Jayanagar, Bangalore 560 011
Sanas Plaza, 1302 Baji Rao Road, Pune 411 002
8 Camac Street, Kolkata 700 017
Ashok Rajpath, Patna 800 004
Chowk, Varanasi 221 001

PRINTED AT INDIA
AND PUBLISHED BY NARENDRA PRAKASH JAIN FOR
MOTILAL BANARSIDASS PUBLISHERS PRIVATE LIMITED,
BUNGALOW ROAD, DELHI 110 007

Contents

Publisher's Note

The passages in this volume are taken from works by Krishnamurti. These include public talks, questions and answers, conversations, and writings.

Krishnamurti always spoke from such a large perspective that his whole vision was implied in any extended passage, or sometimes by even a very short quote. But if one wishes to see how a statement flows out of his whole discourse, one can find the context by referring to the source indicated with each extract. Doing so may be invaluable for deeper comprehension of the passages. With that in mind, a bibliography is provided at the end of the volume for your reference.

Talking things over together as two friends...

In a few days we are going to have discussions, and we can start those discussions this morning. But if you assert and I assert, if you stick to your opinion, to your dogma, to your experience, to your knowledge, and I stick to mine, then there can be no real discussion because neither of us is free to inquire. To discuss is not to share our experiences with each other. There is no sharing at all; there is only the beauty of truth, which neither you nor I can possess. It is simply there.

To discuss intelligently, there must also be a quality not only of affection but of hesitation. You know, unless you hesitate, you can't inquire. Inquiry means hesitating, finding out for yourself, discovering step by step; and when you do that, then you need not follow anybody, you need not ask for correction or for confirmation of your discovery. But all this demands a great deal of intelligence and sensitivity.

By saying that, I hope I have not stopped you from asking questions! You know, this is like talking things over together as two friends. We are neither asserting nor seeking to dominate each other, but each is talking easily, affably, in an atmosphere of friendly companionship, trying to discover. And in that state of mind we do discover, but I assure you, what we discover has very little importance. The important thing is to discover, and after discovering, to keep going. It is detrimental to stay with what you have discovered, for then your mind is closed, finished. But if you die to what you have discovered the moment you have discovered it, then you can flow like the stream, like a river that has an abundance of water.

Collected Works of J. Krishnamurti, Vol. XV
Saanen, 10th Public Talk, 1st August, 1965

I. An Original Ground from Which All Things Arise

There is an origin, an original ground, from which all things arise...

It is immensely important to know and to understand the depth and beauty of meditation. Man has always been asking, from timeless time, whether there is something beyond all thought, beyond all romantic inventions, beyond all time. He has always been asking: Is there something beyond all this suffering, beyond all this chaos, beyond wars, beyond the battle between human beings? Is there something that is immovable, sacred, utterly pure, untouched by any thought, by any experience? This has been the enquiry of serious people, from the ancient of days. To find that out, to come upon it, meditation is necessary. Not the repetitive meditation, that is utterly meaningless. There is a creative energy which is truly religious when the mind is free from all conflict, from all the travail of thought. To come upon that which has no beginning, no end—that is the real depth of meditation and the beauty of it. That requires freedom from all conditioning.

There is complete security in compassionate intelligence—total security. But we want security in ideas, in beliefs, in concepts, in ideals; we hold on to them; they are our security, however false, however irrational. Where there is compassion, with its supreme intelligence, there is security if one is seeking security. Actually where there is compassion, where there is that intelligence, there is no question of security. So there is an origin, an original ground, from which all things arise, and that original ground is not the word. The word is never the thing. And meditation is to come upon that ground which is the origin of all things and which is free from all time. This is the way of meditation. And blessed is he who finds it.

The Flame Of Attention, pp. 30-31

Meditation was like that river, only it had no beginning and no ending...

It was really a marvellous river—wide, deep, with so many cities on its banks, so carelessly free and never abandoning itself. All life was there upon its banks, green fields, forests, solitary houses, death, love, and destruction; there were long, wide bridges over it, graceful and well-used. Other streams and rivers joined it, but she was the mother of all rivers, the little ones and the big ones. She was always full, ever purifying herself, and of an evening it was a blessing to watch her, with deepening colour in the clouds and her waters golden. But the little trickle so far away, amongst those gigantic rocks which seemed so concentrated in producing it, was the beginning of life, and its ending was beyond its banks and the seas.

Meditation was like that river, only it had no beginning and no ending; it began and its ending was its beginning. There was no cause and its movement was its renewal. It was always new, it never gathered to become old, it never got sullied for it had no roots in time. It is good to meditate, not forcing it, not making any effort, beginning with a trickle and going beyond time and space, where thought and feeling cannot enter, where experience is not.

Krishnamurti's Notebook, pp. 226-7

Meditation is a movement in and of the unknown...

Meditation is a movement in and of the unknown. You are not there, only the movement. You are too petty or too great for this movement. It has nothing behind it or in front of it. It is that energy which thought-matter cannot touch. Thought is perversion, for it is the product of yesterday; it is caught in the toils of centuries and so is confused, unclear. Do what you will, the known cannot reach out for the unknown. Meditation is the dying to the known.

KFA BULLETIN, # 4, 1969, p. 9

Without meditation the heart becomes a desert...

The sun came up in a clear sky; you couldn't see it for there were many chimneys in the way, but its radiance filled the sky; and the flowers on the little terrace seemed to come to life, and their colour became more brilliant and intense. It was a beautiful morning, full of light and the sky became a marvellous blue. Meditation included that blue and those flowers; they were part of it; they wound their way through it; they were not a distraction. There's no distraction really, for meditation is not concentration, which is exclusion, a cutting off, a resistance, and so a conflict. A meditative mind can concentrate, which then is not an exclusion, a resistance; but a concentrated mind cannot meditate. It's curious how all-important meditation becomes; there's no end to it, nor is there a beginning to it. It's like a raindrop; in that drop are all the streams, the great rivers, the seas and the waterfalls; that drop nourishes the earth and man; without it, the earth would be a desert. Without meditation the heart becomes a desert, a wasteland. Meditation has its own movement; you can't direct it, shape it, or force it; if you do, it ceases to be meditation. This movement ceases if you are merely an observer, if you are the experiencer. Meditation is the movement that destroys the observer, the experiencer; it's a movement that is beyond all symbol, thought, and feeling. Its rapidity is not measurable.

Krishnamurti's Notebook, pp. 90-1

Meditation is the movement of love...

Meditation is one of the most extraordinary things, and if you do not know what it is, you are like the blind man in a world of bright colour, shadows, and moving light. It is not an intellectual affair, but when the heart enters into the mind, the mind has quite a different quality: it is really, then, limitless, not only in its capacity to think, to act efficiently, but also in its sense of living in a vast space where you are part of everything. Meditation is the movement of love. It isn't the love of the one or of the many. It is like water that anyone can drink out of any jar, whether golden or earthenware; it is inexhaustible. And a peculiar thing takes place which no drug or self-hypnosis can bring about; it is as though the mind enters into itself, beginning at the surface and penetrating ever more deeply, until depth and height have lost their meaning and every form of measurement ceases. In this state there is complete peace, not contentment which has come about through gratification, but a peace that has order, beauty, and intensity. It can all be destroyed, as you can destroy a flower, and yet because of its very vulnerability, it is indestructible. This meditation cannot be learned from another. You must begin without knowing anything about it, and move from innocence to innocence.

The soil in which the meditative mind can begin is the soil of everyday life, the strife, the pain, and the fleeting joy. It must begin there, and bring order, and from there move endlessly. But if you are concerned only with making order, then that very order will bring about its own limitation, and the mind will be its prisoner. In all this movement you must somehow begin from the other end, from the other shore, and not always be concerned with this shore or how to cross the river. You must take a plunge into the water, not knowing how to swim. And the beauty of meditation is that you never know where you are, where you are going, what the end is.

Meditations, 1969, p. 5

II. Traditional Meditation

What you begin with is also what you end up with...

Question: What system of meditation should I follow?

Krishnamurti: At the beginning of your practice, you have both the beginning and the ending of that practice; that is, what you begin with is also what you end up with; the beginning is the end. If I practice, if I copy, I will end up as an imitator, as a machine repeating. If my mind is only capable of repeating, practicing day after day a certain method, following a certain system, at the end my mind is still copying, imitating, repeating. Surely this is obvious, is this not? Therefore at the beginning, I have set the course which the mind shall follow; if I do not understand at the beginning, I shall not understand at the end. That is the obvious truth.

So, I have discovered that the end is at the beginning. Systems through promises, through pleasure, rewards, punishments, make the mind mechanical, stupid, drunk. And at the beginning there is no freedom, and therefore there is no freedom at the end. The beginning matters enormously.

Madras, 12th Public Talk, 10th February 1952

A system of meditation is not meditation...

A system of meditation is not meditation. A system implies a method which you practise in order to achieve something at the end. Something practised over and over again becomes mechanical, does it not? How can a mechanical mind—which has been trained and twisted, tortured to comply to the pattern of what it calls meditation, hoping to achieve a reward at the end—be free to observe, to learn?

There are various schools, in India and further East, where they teach methods of meditation; it is really most appalling. It means training the mind mechanically; it therefore ceases to be free and does not understand the problem.

So when we use the word *meditation* we do not mean something that is practised. We have no method. Meditation means awareness—to be aware of what you are doing, what you are thinking, what you are feeling, aware without any choice, to observe, to learn. Meditation is to be aware of one's conditioning—how one is conditioned by the society in which one lives, in which one has been brought up, by the religious propaganda—aware without any choice, without distortion, without wishing it were different. Out of this awareness comes attention, the capacity to be completely attentive. Then there is freedom to see things as they actually are, without distortion. The mind becomes unconfused, clear, sensitive; such meditation brings about a quality of the mind that is completely silent—of which quality one can go on talking, but it will have no meaning unless it exists.

Beyond Violence, p. 167

Concentration does not lead to the joy of meditation...

Let us differentiate between concentration and meditation. Now when you talk of meditation, most of you mean the mere learning of the trick of concentration. But concentration does not lead to the joy of meditation. Consider what happens in what you call meditation, which is merely the process of training the mind to concentrate on a particular object or idea. You exclude from your mind all other thoughts or images except the one which you have deliberately chosen; you try to focus your mind on that one idea, picture, or word. Now that is merely contraction of thought, limitation of thought. When other thoughts arise during this process of contraction, you dismiss them, you brush them aside. So your mind becomes more and more narrow, less and less elastic, less and less free.

Why do you want to concentrate? Because you see an enticement, a reward, awaiting you as the result of concentration. You want to become a disciple, you want to find the Master, you want to develop spiritually, you want to understand truth. So your concentration becomes utterly destructive of thought and emotion because you consider meditation, concentration, in terms of gain, in terms of escape from turmoil. Just think about it for a moment, those of you who have practised meditation, concentration, for years. You have been forcing your mind to adjust itself to a particular pattern, to conform itself to a particular image or idea, to shape itself according to a particular idiosyncrasy or prejudice. Now, all beliefs, ideals, idiosyncrasies depend on personal like and dislike. Your self-discipline, your so-called meditation, is merely a process by which you try to obtain something in return. And this assurance of something in return, this looking for a reward, also accounts for the large membership of churches and religious societies: these institutions promise a reward, a recompense to their followers who faithfully adhere to their discipline.

Where there is control, there is no meditation of the heart. When you are searching with an eye to gain, to recompense, your search has already ended.

Adyar, 4th Public Talk, 1st January 1934

Professional meditators tell us to control...

The professional mediators tell us to control. Now control implies not only the one who controls but also the thing controlled. As you watch your mind, your thought wanders off and you pull it back; then it wanders again and again you pull it back. So this game goes on endlessly. And if, at the end of ten years or whatever it is, you can control so completely that your mind does not wander at all and has no thoughts whatever, then, it is said, you will have achieved a most extraordinary state. But actually, on the contrary, you will not have achieved anything at all. Control implies resistance.

You Are The World, p. 167

The controller is surely that entity which has determined to practise the method...

Most of us try to control our responses, our reactions; we try to suppress or to shape our desires. In this there is always the controller and the controlled. One never asks who is the controller, and what is that which one is trying to control in so-called meditation? Who is the controller who tries to control his thoughts, his ways of thinking and so on? Who is the controller? The controller surely is that entity which has determined to practice the method or system. Now who is that entity? That entity is from the past, is thought based on reward and punishment. So the controller is of the past and is trying to control his thoughts; but the controller is the controlled. Look, this is all so simple really. When you are envious, you separate envy from yourself. You say, 'I must control envy, I must suppress it'— or you rationalize it. But you are not separate from envy, you are envy. Envy is not separate from you. And yet we play this trick of trying to control envy as though it were something separate from us. So, can you live a life without a single control?—which does not mean indulging in whatever you want. Please put this question to yourself: Can you live a life which is at present so disastrous, so mechanical, so repetitive, without a single sense of control? That can only happen when you perceive with complete clarity, when you give your attention to every thought that arises, not just indulge in thought. When you give such complete attention then you will find out that you can live without the conflict which arises from control. Do you know what that means to have a mind that has understood control and lives without a single shadow of conflict? It means complete freedom. And one must have that complete freedom to come upon that which is eternally true.

The Flame Of Attention, pp. 27-8

Prayer, concentration, and meditation...

Question: Is not the longing expressed in prayer a way to God?

Krishnamurti: First of all, we are going to examine the problems contained in this question. In it are implied prayer, concentration, and meditation. Now, what do we mean by prayer? First of all, in prayer there is petition, supplication to what you call God, reality. You, as an individual, are demanding, petitioning, begging, seeking guidance from something which you call God; therefore your approach is one of seeking a reward, seeking a gratification. You are in trouble, national or individual, and you pray for guidance; or you are confused and you beg for clarity; you look for help to what you call God. In this is implied that God, whatever God may be—we won't discuss that for the moment—is going to clear up the confusion which you and I have created. After all, it is we who have brought about the confusion, the misery, the chaos, the appalling tyranny, the lack of love, and we want what we call God to clear it up. In other words, we want our confusion, our misery, our sorrow, our conflict, to be cleared away by somebody else; we petition another to bring us light and happiness.

Now when you pray, when you beg, petition for something, it generally comes into being. When you ask, you receive; but what you receive will not create order because what you receive does not bring clarity, understanding. It only satisfies, gives gratification, but does not bring about understanding because when you demand, you receive that which you yourself project. How can reality, God, answer your particular demand? Can the immeasurable, the unutterable, be concerned with our petty little worries, miseries, confusions, which we ourselves have created? Therefore what is it that answers? Obviously the immeasurable cannot answer the measured, the petty, the small. But what is it that answers? At the moment when we pray we are fairly silent, in a state of receptivity; then our own subconscious brings a momentary clarity. You want something, you are longing for it, and in that moment of longing, of obsequious begging, you are fairly receptive; your conscious, active mind is comparatively still, so the unconscious projects itself into that and you have an answer. It is surely not an answer from reality, from the immeasurable—it is your own unconscious responding. So don't let us be confused and think that when your prayer is answered you are in relationship with reality. Reality must come to you; you cannot go to it.

In this problem of prayer there is another factor involved—the response of that which we call the inner voice. As I said, when the mind is supplicating, petitioning, it is comparatively still; when you hear the inner voice, it is your own voice projecting itself into that comparatively still mind. Again, how can it be the voice of reality? A mind that is confused, ignorant, craving, demanding, petitioning—how can it understand reality? The mind can receive reality only when it is absolutely still, not demanding, not craving, not longing, not asking, whether for yourself, for the nation or for another. When the mind is absolutely still, when desire ceases, then only reality comes into being. A person who is demanding, petitioning, supplicating, longing for direction will find what he seeks, but it will not be the truth. What he receives will be the response of the unconscious layers of his own mind which project themselves into the conscious; that still, small voice which directs him is not the real but only the response of the unconscious.

The First And Last Freedom, pp. 216-7

The understanding of beauty is part of meditation...

What has beauty to do with a religious mind? You might ask why all the religious traditions and the rituals never referred to beauty. But the understanding of beauty is part of meditation, not the beauty of a woman or a man or the beauty of a face, which has its own beauty, but about beauty itself, the actual essence of beauty. Most monks, *sanyasis*, and the so-called religiously inclined minds totally disregard this and become hardened towards their environment. Once it happened that we were staying in the Himalayas with some friends; there was a group of sanyasis in front of us, going down the path, chanting; they never looked at the trees, never looked at the beauty of the earth, the beauty of the blue sky, the birds, the flowers, the running waters; they were totally concerned with their own salvation, with their own entertainment. And that custom, that tradition, has been going on for a thousand years. A man who is supposed to be religious must shun, put aside, all beauty, and his life becomes dull, without any aesthetic sense; yet beauty is one of the delights of truth.

... When we see a marvellous mountain, snowcapped against the blue sky and the deep shadowed valleys, that great grandeur and majesty absorb us completely; for a moment we are completely silent because its majesty takes us over, we forget ourselves. Beauty is where 'you' are not. The essence of beauty is the absence of the self. The essence of meditation is to enquire into the abnegation of the self.

The Flame Of Attention, pp. 23-5

III. Coming to Meditation Anew

How am I to meditate?

You are always asking the 'how'—'How am I to meditate?' That is one of the childish questions you can ask about something which is so immense—to ask somebody, 'Tell me what to do, tell me how to hold the earth in one's hand, tell me how to hold the sea or the air in one's fist'. And if you observe, that is what you all want. You want to experience something through a method. A method implies not only conformity, not only measurement of achievement, but a method implies a system or a path to a fixed point, doesn't it? It is there, all that you do is to practice. It is most illogical, irrational, without any meaning whatsoever, because if you observe in your life, there is nothing stable, nothing permanent. You may want it, you may want a permanent relationship with your wife, with your children, with your neighbour, with your society.

You cannot have anything permanent. Even your bank account is not permanent. No relationship is permanent. Everything is in a flux, is in movement, and realizing this consciously or unconsciously, we want something permanent, something that we can hold on to. And that we call truth, God, or what you like. So if you really understand, see the fact, see the truth that reality has no resting place; it is like being in an uncharted sea, you have to find your way to it—not your way or somebody else's way—but you have to find it.

And when you have a path leading to a reality—in that is implied time. To reach from here to there you require time, many days to travel, to cross the distance. And in that lag of time between here and there, there are other factors coming in. Therefore you say, 'Let me concentrate, think on that one thing and reject everything else, subjugate everything else to that one factor . The mechanical process of system brings about insensitivity, suppression, resistance against what you are actually, imposing on what you are something you think what ought to be; and there is conflict, battle. You want to control, you want to suppress, you discipline, force yourself to sit quietly, to breathe rightly, do all those fantastic things, hoping that you will eventually reach something about which you know absolutely nothing. So a wise man rejects the whole system, the whole idea, concept, of systems altogether, because they don't lead anywhere.

Krishnamurti In India 1970-71, p. 173

An awareness without choice...

Meditation is this attention in which there is an awareness, without choice, of the movement of all things—the cawing of the crows, the electric saw ripping through the wood, the trembling of leaves, the noisy stream, a boy calling, the feelings, the motives, the thoughts chasing each other and going deeper, the awareness of total consciousness. And in this attention, time as yesterday pursuing into the space of tomorrow and the twisting and turning of consciousness has become quiet and still. In this stillness there is an immeasurable, not comparable movement, a movement that has no being; that's the essence of bliss and death and life. A movement that cannot be followed for it leaves no path and because it is still, motionless; it is the essence of all motion.

Krishnamurti's Notebook, p. 64

I want to see what is in the cupboard of my mind...

Questioner: It is very difficult not to analyse.

Krishnamurti: When you are analysing, you are not looking.

Questioner: I know.

Krishnamurti: You don't know; otherwise, you wouldn't analyse. Look, I want to see what is in the cupboard of my mind, what is stored up there; I want to read all the things it contains because the content of the mind is the mind. I want to see what I am during the waking hours, walking, talking, making gestures, when I am at the office, when I am angry, in the fleeting moments of pleasure and sex, and the delight of seeing the hills, the streams, the trees, the birds and the clouds. But I also want to see myself when I am asleep, be aware of what is going on. Don't you want to see yourself, awake and asleep? You think you do. Do you know what it means to learn about yourself? It means hard work, daily observation, watching, watching, watching, but not self-centred watching, just watching, like you watch a bird, or the movement of a cloud; you can't change the movement of the cloud, so just watch in the same way.

The Awakening Of Intelligence, pp. 315-6

The very inquiry into what is meditation will open the door to meditation...

The question is not *how to meditate*, what system to follow, but *what is meditation*? The *how* can only produce what the method offers, but the very inquiry into what is meditation will open the door to meditation. The inquiry does not lie outside of the mind, but within the movement of the mind itself. In pursuing that inquiry, what becomes all-important is to understand the seeker himself, and not what he seeks. What he seeks is the projection of his own craving, of his own compulsions, desires. When this fact is seen, all searching ceases, which in itself is enormously significant. Then the mind is no longer grasping at something beyond itself, there is no outward movement with its reaction inwards; but when seeking has entirely stopped, there is a movement of the mind which is neither outward nor inward. Seeking does not come to an end by any act of will, or by a complex process of conclusions. To stop seeking demands great understanding. The ending of search is the beginning of a still mind.

Commentaries On Living Series II, pp. 218-9

Meditation is not a search...

Meditation is not a search; it's not a seeking, a probing, an exploration. It is an explosion and discovery. It's not the taming of the brain to conform, nor is it a self-introspective analysis; it is certainly not the training in concentration which includes, chooses, and denies. It's something that comes naturally, when all positive and negative assertions and accomplishments have been understood and drop away easily. It is the total emptiness of the brain. It's the emptiness that is essential, not what's in the emptiness; there is seeing only from emptiness; all virtue, not social morality and respectability, springs from it. It's out of this emptiness love comes, otherwise it's not love. Foundation of righteousness is in this emptiness. It's the end and beginning of all things.

Looking out of the window, as Orion was climbing higher and higher, the brain was intensely alive and sensitive; and meditation became something entirely different, something which the brain could not cope with and so fell back upon itself and became silent. The hours till dawn and after seemed to have had no beginning and as the sun came up, the mountains and the clouds caught its first rays and there was astonishment in splendour. And day began. Strangely meditation went on.

Krishnamurti's Notebook, pp. 68-9

In the flame of meditation, thought ends...

There on the perfumed verandah, when dawn was still far away and the trees were still silent, what is essence is beauty. But this essence is not experienceable; experiencing must cease, for experience only strengthens the known. The known is never the essence. Meditation is never the further experiencing; it is not only the ending of experience, which is the response to challenge, great or small, but it is the opening of the door to essence, opening the door of a furnace whose fire utterly destroys, without leaving any ashes; there are no remains. We are the remains, the yes-sayers of many thousand yesterdays, a continuous series of endless memories, of choice and despair. The big self and the little self are the pattern of existence and existence is thought and thought is existence, with never ending sorrow. In the flame of meditation thought ends and with it feeling, for neither is love. Without love, there is no essence; without it there are only ashes on which is based our existence. Out of the emptiness love is.

Krishnamurti's Notebook, pp. 170-1

Meditation is a movement without any motive, without words and the activity of thought...

Words cannot measure the expanse, the rolling hills and the vast space, nor the blue sky and the distant desert. It was the whole earth. One hardly dared to talk, there was such compelling silence, not to be disturbed. And that silence cannot be measured by words. If you were a poet, you would probably measure it with words, put it into a poem, but that which is written is not the actual. The word is not the thing. And here, sitting beside a rock which was becoming warm, man did not exist. The rolling hills, the higher mountains, the great sweeping valleys, deep in blue—there was no you, there was nothing but that.

From ancient times all civilizations have had this concept of measurement. All their marvellous buildings were based on mathematical measurement. When you look at the Acropolis and the glory of the Parthenon and the hundred and ten floor buildings of New York, they have all had to have this measurement.

Measurement is not only by the rule; measurement exists in the very brain—the tall and the short, the better, the more. This comparative process has existed for time beyond time. We are always comparing. The passing of examinations from school, college, university—our whole way of living has become a series of calculated measurements: the beautiful and the ugly, the noble and ignoble—one's whole set of values, the arguments that end in conclusions, the power of people, the power of nations. Measurement has been necessary to man. And the brain, being conditioned to measurement, to comparison, tries to measure the immeasurable—measuring with words that which cannot ever be measured. It has been a long process for centuries upon centuries—the greater gods and the lesser gods, measuring the vast expanse of the universe and measuring the speed of the athlete. This comparison has brought a great many fears and sorrows.

Now, on that rock, a lizard has come to warm itself quite close to us. You can see its black eyes, its scaly back and the long tail. It is so still, motionless. The sun has made that rock quite warm, and the lizard, coming out of its cold night and warming itself, is waiting for some fly or insect to come along—it will measure the distance and snap it up.

To live without comparison is to live without any kind of measurement inwardly, never to compare what you are with what you should be. The word *meditation* means not only to ponder, to think over, to probe, to look, to weigh; it also has a much deeper meaning in Sanskrit—to measure, which is 'to become'. In meditation there must be no measurement. This meditation must not be a conscious meditation in deliberately chosen postures. This meditation must be totally unconscious, never knowing that you are meditating. If you deliberately meditate, it is another form of desire, as any other expression of desire. The objects may vary; your meditation may be to reach the highest, but the motive is the desire to achieve, as the business man, as the builder of a great cathedral. Meditation is a movement without any motive, without words and the activity of thought. It must be something that is not deliberately set about. Only then is meditation a movement in the infinite, measureless to man, without a goal, without an end and without a beginning. And that has a strange action in daily life, because all life is one and then becomes sacred. And that which is sacred can never be killed. To kill another is unholy. It cries to heaven as a bird kept in a cage. One never realizes how sacred life is, not only your little life but the lives of millions of others, from the things of nature to extraordinary human beings. And in meditation which is without measurement, there is the very action of that which is most noble, most sacred and holy.

Krishnamurti To Himself, pp. 81-3

Meditation is the attention in which there is no registration...

Meditation is the attention in which there is no registration. Normally the brain is registering almost everything—the noise, the words which are being used—it is registering like a tape. Now is it possible for the brain not to register except that which is absolutely necessary? Why should I register an insult? Why? Why should I register flattery? It is unnecessary. Why should I register any hurts? Unnecessary. Therefore, register only that which is necessary in order to operate in daily life—as a technician, a writer and so on—but psychologically, do not register anything. In meditation there is no registration psychologically, no registration except the practical facts of living, going to the office, working in a factory and so on—nothing else. Out of that comes complete silence, because thought has come to an end—except to function only where it is absolutely necessary. Time has come to an end, and there is a totally different kind of movement, in silence.

The Wholeness Of Life, p. 144

Self-knowing is the beginning of meditation...

There was not a sound in the valley; it was dark and there wasn't a leaf moving; dawn would come in an hour or so.

Meditation is not self-hypnosis, by words or thought, by repetition or image; all imagination of every kind must be put aside, for they lead to delusion. The understanding of facts and not theories, not the pursuits of conclusions and adjustments to them and the ambitions of visions—all these must be set aside; and meditation is the understanding of these facts and so going beyond them. Self-knowing is the beginning of meditation; otherwise, so-called meditation leads to every form of immaturity and silliness.

It was early and the valley was asleep. On waking, meditation was the continuation of what had been going on; the body was without a movement; it was not made to be quiet but it was quiet; there was no thought but the brain was watchful, without any sensation; neither feeling nor thought existed. And a timeless movement began. Word is time, indicating space; word is of the past or the future, but the active present has no word. The dead can be put into words, but the living cannot. Every word used to communicate about the living is the denial of the living. It was a movement that passed through and between the walls of the brain, but the brain had no contact with it; it was incapable of pursuit or of recognition. This movement was something that was not born out of the known; the brain could follow the known as it could recognize it, but here no recognition of any kind was possible. A movement has direction but this had no direction; it was not static. Because it was without direction, it was the essence of action. All direction is of influence or of reaction. But action which is not the outcome of reaction, push or pull, is total energy. This energy, love, has its own movement. But the word *love,* the known, is not love. There is only the fact, the freedom from the known. Meditation was the explosion of the fact.

Krishnamurti's Notebook, pp. 181-2

You should meditate only in solitude...

It was one of those lovely mornings that have never been before. The sun was just coming up and you saw it between the eucalyptus and the pine. It was over the waters, golden, burnished with such light that exists only between the mountains and the sea. It was such a clear morning, breathless, full of that strange light that one sees not only with one's eyes but with one's heart. And when you see it, the heavens are very close to earth, and you are lost in the beauty. You know, you should never meditate in public, or with another, or in a group; you should meditate only in solitude, in the quiet of the night or in the still, early morning. When you meditate in solitude, it must be solitude. You must be completely alone, not following a system, a method, repeating words, or pursuing a thought, or shaping a thought according to your desire.

This solitude comes when the mind is freed from thought. When there are influences of desire or of the things that the mind is pursuing, either in the future or in the past, there is no solitude. Only in the immensity of the present this aloneness comes. And then, in quiet secrecy in which all communication has come to an end, in which there is no observer with his anxieties, with his stupid appetites and problems—only then, in that quiet aloneness, meditation becomes something that cannot be put into words. Then meditation is an eternal movement.

I don't know if you have ever meditated, if you have ever been alone, by yourself, far away from everything, from every person, from every thought and pursuit. If you have ever been completely alone, not isolated, not withdrawn into some fanciful dream or vision, but far away, so that in yourself there is nothing recognizable, nothing that you touch by thought or feeling, so far away that in this full solitude the very silence becomes the only flower, the only light, and the timeless quality that is not measurable by thought—only in such meditation love has its being. Don't bother to express it; it will express itself. Don't use it. Don't try to put it into action; it will act, and when it acts, in that action there is no regret, no contradiction, none of the misery and travail of man.

So meditate alone. Get lost. And don't try to remember where you have been. If you try to remember it, then it will be something that is dead. And if you hold on to the memory of it, then you will never be alone again. So meditate in that endless solitude, in the beauty of that love, in that innocency, in the new; then there is the bliss that is imperishable.

The sky is very blue, the blue that comes after the rain, and these rains have come after many months of drought. After the rain the skies are washed clean and the hills are rejoicing, and the earth is still. And every leaf has the light of the sun on it, and the feeling of the earth is very close to you. So meditate in the very secret recesses of your heart and mind, where you have never been before.

Meditations, 1969, pp. 8-9

There is no tomorrow in meditation...

Meditation without a set formula, without a cause and reason, without end and purpose is an incredible phenomenon. It is not only a great explosion which purifies but also it is death, that has no tomorrow. Its purity devastates, leaving no hidden corner where thought can lurk in its own dark shadows. Its purity is vulnerable; it is not a virtue brought into being through resistance. It is pure because it has no resistance, like love. There is no tomorrow in meditation, no argument with death. The death of yesterday and of tomorrow does not leave the petty present of time, and time is always petty, but a destruction that is the new. Meditation is this, not the silly calculations of the brain in search of security. Meditation is destruction to security, and there is great beauty in meditation, not the beauty of the things that have been put together by man or by nature but of silence. This silence is emptiness in which and from which all things flow and have their being. It is unknowable, neither intellect nor feeling can make their way to it; there is no way to it and a method to it is the invention of a greedy brain. All the ways and means of the calculating self must be destroyed wholly; all going forward or backward, the way of time, must come to an end, without tomorrow. Meditation is destruction: it's a danger to those who wish to lead a superficial life and a life of fancy and myth.

Krishnamurti's Notebook, pp. 81-2

IV. Suggestions to Young People

See if you can keep your eyes from moving...

First of all sit absolutely still. Sit comfortably, cross your legs, sit absolutely still, close your eyes, and see if you can keep your eyes from moving. You understand? Your eye balls are apt to move, keep them completely quiet, for fun. Then, as you sit very quietly, find out what your thought is doing. Watch it as you watched the lizard. Watch thought, the way it runs, one thought after another. So you begin to learn, to observe.

Are you watching your thoughts—how one thought pursues another thought, thought saying, 'This is a good thought, this is a bad thought'? When you go to bed at night, and when you walk, watch your thought. Just watch thought, do not correct it, and then you will learn the beginning of meditation. Now sit very quietly. Shut your eyes and see that the eyeballs do not move at all. Then watch your thoughts so that you learn. Once you begin to learn there is no end to learning.

Krishnamurti On Education, pp. 23-4

Krishnamurti: ... Do you know anything about meditation?

Student: No, Sir.

Krishnamurti: But the older people do not know either. They sit in a corner, close their eyes and concentrate, like school boys trying to concentrate on a book. That is not meditation. Meditation is something extraordinary, if you know how to do it. I am going to talk a little about it.

First of all, sit very quietly; do not force yourself to sit quietly, but sit or lie down quietly without force of any kind. Do you understand?

Then watch your thinking. Watch what you are thinking about. You find you are thinking about your shoes, your saris, what you are going to say, the bird outside to which you listen: follow such thoughts and enquire why each thought arises. Do not try to change your thinking. See why certain thoughts arise in your mind so that you begin to understand the meaning of every thought and every feeling without any enforcement. And when a thought arises, do not condemn it, do not say it is right, it is wrong, it is good, it is bad. Just watch it, so that you begin to have a perception, a consciousness which is active in seeing every kind of thought, every kind of feeling. You will know every hidden secret thought, every hidden motive, every feeling, without distortion, without saying it is right, wrong, good, or bad. When you look, when you go into thought very, very deeply, your mind becomes extraordinarily subtle, alive. No part of the mind is asleep. The mind is completely awake.

That is merely the foundation. Then your mind is very quiet. Your whole being becomes very still. Then go through that stillness, deeper, further—that whole process is meditation. Meditation is not to sit in a corner repeating a lot of words, or to think of a picture and go into some wild, ecstatic imaginings.

To understand the whole process of your thinking and feeling is to be free from all thought, to be free from all feeling so that your mind, your whole being becomes very quiet. And that is also part of life, and with that quietness you can look at the tree, you can look at people, you can look at the sky and the stars. That is the beauty of life.

Krishnamurti On Education, pp. 58-60

Every thought has a significance...

Every thought has a significance; and if the mind is incapable of seeing the significance, not just of one or two thoughts, but of each thought as it arises, then merely to concentrate on a particular idea, image, or set of words—which is generally called meditation—is a form of self-hypnosis.

So, whether you are sitting quietly, talking, or playing, are you aware of the significance of every thought, of every reaction that you happen to have? Try it and you will see how difficult it is to be aware of every movement of your own thought, because thoughts pile up so quickly one on top of another. But if you want to examine every thought, if you really want to see the content of it, then you will find that your thoughts slow down and you can watch them. This slowing down of thinking and the examining of every thought is the process of meditation; and if you go into it you will find that, by being aware of every thought, your mind—which is now a vast storehouse of restless thoughts all battling against each other—becomes very quiet, completely still. There is then no urge, no compulsion, no fear in any form; and, in this stillness, that which is true comes into being. There is no 'you' who experiences truth, but the mind being still, truth comes into it. The moment there is a 'you' there is the experiencer, and the experiencer is merely the result of thought; he has no basis without thinking.

Think On These Things, pp. 189-90

Go to the very end of that thought and finish it...

Questioner: Where does silence come in then?

Krishnamurti: You don't bother about silence because if thought is coming in, you are not silent. Then don't force yourself to be quiet; pursue that thought.

Questioner: Is there any end to that?

Krishnamurti: Yes, if you finish it; but if you don't go to the very end of it, it will come back because you haven't finished one thing. You have understood?

Look, I come out of the house, go round the lawn and watch, pay attention to the beauty, the tenderness, the movement of the leaf. I watch everything and I come into the room and sit. You read something and I sit quietly. I am trying to sit quietly and my body jerks because I have a habit of twitching, so I have to watch that, I pay attention to it, I don't correct it. You can't correct the movement of the leaf can you? So in the same way I don't want to correct the movement of my hands; I watch it, I pay attention to it. When you pay attention to it, it becomes quiet—try it. I sit quietly, one second, two seconds, ten seconds, then suddenly up pops a thought, 'I have to go to some place this afternoon. I didn't do my exercises, I didn't clean the bath'. Or sometimes the thought is much more complicated, 'I am envious of that man'. Now I feel that envy. So go to the very end of that and look at it. Envy implies comparison, competition, imitation. Do I want to imitate?—you follow? Go to the very end of that thought and finish it; don't carry it over. And when another thought pops up, you say, 'Wait, I'll come back to that'.

If you want to play this game very carefully, you write every thought you have on a piece of paper and you will soon find out how thought can be orderly because you are finishing every thought, one after the other. And when you sit quietly the next day, you are really quiet. No thought pops up because you have finished with it; which means you have polished your shoes, you have cleaned your bath tub, you have put the towel in its right place at the right moment. You don't say when you sit down, 'I didn't put the towel back'. So the thing that you are doing is finished each time, and when you sit quietly you are marvellously quiet, you bring an extraordinary sense of orderliness into your life. If you haven't that orderliness, you cannot be silent; and when you have it, when the mind is really quiet, then there is real beauty and the mystery of things begins. That is real religion.

Beginnings Of Learning, pp. 101-3

Can you watch without the watcher?...

When you sit very quietly, or lie down very quietly, the body is completely relaxed, isn't it? Have you ever tried to sit very, very quietly? Not to force it, because the moment you force it, it is finished. To sit very quietly, either with your eyes closed or open. If you have your eyes open there is a little more distraction, you begin to see things. So, after looking at things, the curve of the tree, the leaves, the bushes, after looking at it all with care, then close your eyes. Then you will not say to yourself, 'What's happening, let me look'. First look at everything—the furniture, the colour of the chair, the colour of the sweater; look at the shape of the tree. After having looked, the desire to look out is less. I've seen that blue sky and I've finished with it and I won't look again. But you must first look. Then you can sit quietly. When you sit quietly, or lie down very quietly, the blood flows easily into your head, doesn't it? There is no strain. That's why they say you must sit cross-legged with head very straight, because the blood flows easier that way. If you sit crouched it is more difficult for the blood to go into the head. So you sit or lie down very, very quietly. Don't force it, don't fidget. If you fidget, then watch it; don't say, 'I must not'. Then, when you sit very quietly, you watch your mind. First, you watch the mind. Don't correct it. Don't say, 'This thought is good; that thought is not good'; just watch it. Then you will see that there is a watcher and the watched. There is a division. The moment there is a division, there is conflict.

Now, can you watch without the watcher? Is there a watching without the watcher? It is the watcher that says, 'This is good and that is bad. This I like and that I don't like' or, 'I wish she hadn't said this or that. I wish I had more food'.

To watch without the watcher—try it some time. That's part of meditation. Just begin with that. That's good enough. And you will see, if you have done it, what an extraordinary thing takes place...your body becomes very, very intelligent. Now the body is not intelligent because we have spoiled it. You understand what I mean? We have destroyed the natural intelligence of the body itself. Then you will find that the body says, 'Go to bed at the right time'. It wants it; it has its own intelligence and activity. And also if it wants to be lazy, let it be lazy.

Beginnings Of Learning, pp. 76-7

V. If One's House Is Not in Order...

If one's house is not in order...

We are going into all this so as to bring about order in our life—order in our 'house', which has no order. There is so much disorder in our life; and without establishing an order that is whole, integral, meditation has no meaning whatsoever. If one's 'house' is not in order, one may sit in meditation, hoping that through that meditation one will bring about order; but what happens when one is living in disorder and one meditates? One has fanciful dreams, illusions, and all kinds of nonsensical results. But a sane, intelligent, logical man must first establish order in daily life, then he can go into the depths of meditation, into the meaning and the beauty of it, the greatness of it, the worth of it.

The Network Of Thought, pp. 67-8

One must lay the foundation of righteous behavior...

If one is free from this everlasting search, free from the demand and the desire to experience something extraordinary, then we can proceed to find out what meditation is. That word —like the words *love, death, beauty, happiness*—is so loaded. There are so many schools which teach you how to meditate. But to understand what meditation is, one must lay the foundation of righteous behaviour. Without that foundation, meditation is really a form of self-hypnosis; without being free from anger, jealousy, envy, greed, acquisitiveness, hate, competition, the desire for success—all the moral, respectable forms of what is considered righteous—without laying the right foundation, without actually living a daily life free of the distortion of personal fear, anxiety, greed and so on, meditation has very little meaning. The laying of that foundation is all-important. So one asks: What is virtue? What is morality? Please do not say that this question is bourgeois, that it has no meaning in a society which is permissive, which allows anything. We are not concerned with that kind of society; we are concerned with a life completely free from fear, a life which is capable of deep, abiding love. Without that, meditation becomes a deviation; it is like taking a drug—as so many have done—to have an extraordinary experience and yet leading a shoddy little life. Those who take drugs do have some strange experiences: they see perhaps a little more colour, they become perhaps a little more sensitive, and being sensitive, in that chemical state, they do perhaps see things without space between the 'observer' and the thing observed; but when the chemical effect is over, they are back to where they were with fear, with boredom, back again in the old routine—so they have to take the drug again.

Unless one lays the foundation of virtue, meditation becomes a trick to control the mind, to make the mind quiet, to force the mind to conform to the pattern of a system that says, 'Do these things and you will have great reward'. But such a mind—do what you will with all the methods and the systems that are offered—will remain small, petty, conditioned, and therefore worthless. One has to inquire into what virtue is, what behaviour is. Is behaviour the result of environmental conditioning, of a society, of a culture in which one has been brought up?—you behave according to that. Is that virtue? Or does virtue lie in freedom from the social morality of greed, envy and all the rest of it?—which is considered highly respectable. Can virtue be cultivated?—and if it can be cultivated, then does it not become a mechanical thing and therefore have no virtue at all? Virtue is something that is living, flowing, that is constantly renewing itself; it cannot possibly be put together in time; it is like suggesting that you can cultivate humility. Can you cultivate humility? It is only the vain man that 'cultivates' humility; whatever he may cultivate he will still remain vain. But in seeing very clearly the nature of vanity and pride, in that very seeing there is freedom from that vanity and pride—and in that there is humility. When this is very clear, then we can proceed to find out what meditation is. If one cannot do this very deeply, in a most real and serious way—not just for one or two days then drop it—please do not talk about meditation. Meditation, if you understand what it is, is one of the most extraordinary things; but you cannot possibly understand it unless you have come to the end of seeking, groping, wanting, greedily clutching at something which you consider truth—which is your own projection. You cannot come to it unless you are no longer demanding 'experience' at all, but are understanding the confusion in which one lives, the disorder of one's own life. In the observation of that disorder, order comes—which is not a blueprint. When you have done this—which in itself is meditation—then we can ask, not only what meditation is but also what meditation is not, because in the denial of that which is false, the truth is.

Flight Of The Eagle, pp. 38-9

There is nothing but the body...

Meditation is never the control of the body. There is no actual division between the organism and the mind. The brain, the nervous system, and the thing we call the mind are all one, indivisible. It is the natural act of meditation that brings about the harmonious movement of the whole. To divide the body from the mind and to control the body with intellectual decisions is to bring about contradiction, from which arise various forms of struggle, conflict, and resistance.

Every decision to control only breeds resistance, even the determination to be aware. Meditation is the understanding of the division brought about by decision. Freedom is not the act of decision but the act of perception. The seeing is the doing. It is not a determination to see and then to act. After all, will is desire with all its contradictions. When one desire assumes authority over another, that desire becomes will. In this there is inevitable division. And meditation is the understanding of desire, not the overcoming of one desire by another. Desire is the movement of sensation, which becomes pleasure and fear. This is sustained by the constant dwelling of thought upon one or the other. Meditation really is a complete emptying of the mind. Then there is only the functioning of the body; there is only the activity of the organism and nothing else; then thought functions without identification as the 'me' and the 'not-me'. Thought is mechanical, as is the organism. What creates conflict is thought identifying itself with one of its parts which becomes the me, the self and the various divisions in that self. There is no need for the self at any time. There is nothing but the body, and freedom of the mind can happen only when thought is not breeding the me. There is no self to understand but only the thought that creates the self. When there is only the organism without the self, perception, both visual and non-visual, can never be distorted. There is only seeing *what is*, and that very perception goes beyond *what is*. The emptying of the mind is not an activity of thought or an intellectual process. The continuous seeing of *what is* without any kind of distortion naturally empties the mind of all thought, and yet that very mind can use thought when it is necessary. Thought is mechanical and meditation is not.

Beginnings Of Learning, pp. 250-1

The four seasons...

Questioner: Will you please explain the idea that one must die each day, or that one must live the four seasons in a day?

Krishnamurti: Is it not essential that there should be a constant renewal, a rebirth? If the present is burdened with the experience of yesterday there can be no renewal. Renewal is not the action of birth and death; it is beyond the opposites; only freedom from the accumulation of memory brings renewal, and there is no understanding save in the present.

Mind can understand the present only if it does not compare, judge; the desire to alter or condemn the present without understanding it gives continuance to the past. Only in comprehending the reflection of the past in the mirror of the present, without distortion, is there renewal.

The accumulation of memory is called knowledge; with this burden, with the scars of experience, thought is ever interpreting the present and so giving continuity to its own scars and conditioning. This continuity is time-binding and so there is no rebirth, no renewal. If you have lived an experience fully, completely, have you not found that it leaves no traces behind? It is only the incomplete experiences that leave their mark, giving continuity to self-identified memory. We consider the present as a means to an end, so the present loses its immense significance. The present is the eternal. But how can a mind that is made up, put together, understand that which is not put together, which is beyond all value, the eternal?

As each experience arises, live it out as fully and deeply as possible; think it out, feel it out extensively and profoundly; be aware of its pain and pleasure, of your judgments and identifications. Only when experience is completed is there a renewal. We must be capable of living the four seasons in a day, to be keenly aware, to experience, to understand, and be free of the gatherings of each day. With the end of each day the mind-heart must empty itself of the accumulation of its pleasures and pains. We gather consciously and unconsciously; it is comparatively easy to discard what has been consciously acquired, but it is more difficult for thought to free itself from the unconscious accumulations, the past, the incompleted experiences with their recurring memories. Thought-feeling clings so tenaciously to what it has gathered because it is afraid to be insecure.

Meditation is renewal, the dying each day to the past; it is an intense passive awareness, the burning away of the desire to continue, to become. As long as mind-heart is self-protecting, there will be continuity without renewal. Only when the mind ceases to create is there creation.

Ojai, 7th Public Talk, 1945

Do not make meditation a complicated affair...

Do not make meditation a complicated affair; it is really very simple, and because it is simple it is very subtle. Its subtlety will escape the mind if the mind approaches it with all kinds of fanciful and romantic ideas. Meditation, really, is a penetration into the unknown; and so the known, the memory, the experience, the knowledge which it has acquired during the day, or during a thousand days, must end. For it is only a free mind that can penetrate into the very heart of the immeasurable. So meditation is both the penetration and the ending of the yesterday. The ending of the yesterday and the penetration into the unknown is not a dual process, nor is it the endless corridor of opposites.

The trouble begins when we ask how to end the yesterday. There is really no 'how'. The 'how' implies a method, a system, and it is this very method and system that has conditioned the mind. Just see the truth of this. Freedom is necessary—not 'how' to be free. The 'how to be free' only enslaves you.

The past is based on imitation, conformity, and obedience to a principle or an ideal. This is the substance of the past ever repeating in the present and making the future. In this vicious circle thought is caught. Thought is the past, and when you ask how to be free from the past, thought is again building the web of time. To see the truth of this, there must be freedom—not at the end but at the very beginning.

KFA BULLETIN, 1977, # 32, pp. 15-16

Meditation is...the awareness of the responses of the conditioned thought to every challenge...

Question: I am troubled by my dreams night after night. Can one not free oneself from this exhausting process?

Krishnamurti: Let us find out together what is the right answer to this problem—together, you and I. Don't listen to me merely as if I am the talker and you the listener; but together we shall find the truth of this because it is your problem.

What do you mean by waking and dreaming? When are you awake? At least, when do we think we are awake? And when do we think we are dreaming? Please, this is not a psychological question. Just follow it step by step, simply. Do not translate it and say, 'Yes, Shankara, Buddha, said so', and then wander away. I am talking very simply about what is the actual fact. When do we think we are awake? When our conscious mind is functioning, is it not? That is, there is the mind that is operating every day, and when that is functioning, we are awake. You are awake when you have a job, when you are studying, when you are getting into the tramcar or into the bus, when you are following, when you are scolding someone, when you are ambitious or sexual or what you will. That is, during the day we think we are awake and when we sleep we think we are in a state when the mind has gone to sleep—rather, has been put to sleep.

Now, is the mind ever asleep? Is it ever at rest? The mind is both the conscious as well as the unconscious. The consciousness shows very little; that which we call the conscious is very superficial; but there is a dreaded part, undiscovered, hidden, below this conscious part, which is the unconscious; and our mind is both the conscious as well as the unconscious. The conscious mind is urged, propelled, driven, or held back by the unconscious. You may think you are outwardly a very peaceful person, that outwardly you are not ambitious; but below, hidden deep down, there is the bellowing going on in your heart—your urges, compulsions, desires, motives. The unconscious is the reservoir of all the past of humanity—not the past of your being only, but of your father, of your fore-fathers, of your nation, of human beings—the racial traditions, the caste prejudices; all that is held in the unconscious.

The conscious mind is occupied during the day with trivial things, and the occupation with those trivial things we call the waking state. When we go to sleep the mind goes on being active, it is still thinking out the problems of the day in relation to and coloured by the unconscious; and when the unconscious wants to put some idea, some impression on the conscious mind which it is not capable of doing during the day, then you have dreams. That is, your conscious mind is occupied throughout the day; it cannot receive new impressions, new promptings, new hints, because it is too occupied; and then you go to sleep, and the unconscious projects into that semi-active conscious mind, its impressions. When you wake up, you say you have had a dream. Then begins the translation of that dream by the conscious mind, and you say you have had a marvellous experience.

So, as long as you are not consciously aware at the time, throughout the waking time, throughout the waking period of the promptings of the unconscious, as long as you are not open to every impression or every hint, from the unconscious, you must continue to dream; there must be a conflict between the conscious and the unconscious. Sirs, these are all very simple facts. If you observe your own being, your own thoughts, your daily activities, if you are aware of them, you will see that this is the actual process going on. There is nothing mysterious about it.

The whole process—the unconscious, the conscious, the promptings, the hints, the impressions, and the translating of all those impulses by the conscious—all that is your being; that is what you are. If you are not open, if the mind is not open to the total process but is only occupied with the part, naturally there must be dreams—dreams being the impressions and the projections of the unconscious. So there is this constant struggle going on between the conscious and the unconscious, because the conscious can never compete completely with the unconscious, because the conscious is trying to translate every impression according to certain demands, activities, and results.

Sirs, it is only when we begin to understand this total process of our being, the actual state in which we are that then there is a possibility of an integrated human being. Surely that is the beginning of meditation, is it not? Meditation is not merely concentration on some idea, on some picture, or the desire to be something—that is just immature, childish; it is not meditation. Meditation is this understanding of the total process, the observation, the awareness of the responses of the conditioned thought to every challenge, so that the mind remains aware of its content, its activity, its pursuits, its hidden motives; so that, through that constant awareness without choice, there is freedom, there is an integration—this whole process is meditation. A mind that is capable of observing without choice, seeing things as they are without trying to interpret them, without translating them, without twisting them, without distorting them—such a mind, through awareness, shall know what peace is, such a mind is capable then of being truly silent. Then only, in that silence, *that which is* comes into being. But the mind that is seeking a result can never find truth.

Poona, 4th Public Talk, 1st February 1953

There is no permanent self about which to learn...

Meditation is the understanding of the whole activity of thought which brings into being the 'me', the self, the ego, as a fact. Then thought tries to understand the image which it has created, as though that self were something permanent. This self again divides itself into the higher and the lower and this division in turn brings conflict, misery and confusion. The knowing of the self is one thing, and the understanding of how the self comes into being is another. One presupposes the existence of the self as a permanent entity. The other, through observation, learns how the self is put together by thought. So the understanding of thought, its ways and its subtleties, its activities and its divisions, is the beginning of meditation. But if you consider the self a permanent entity, you are studying a self which is non-existent, for it is merely a bundle of memories, words, and experiences. So self-knowing is not the knowledge of the self but seeing how the self has been put together and how this makes for the fragmentation of life. One must see very clearly this misunderstanding. There is no permanent self about which to learn. But learning about the ways of thought and its activities is to dissipate self-centred activity. This is the foundation of meditation. Without understanding this deeply and radically, meditation becomes merely a game for the foolish, with their absurd little visions, fanciful experiences, and the mischief of power. This foundation implies awareness, the observation of *what is* without any choice, to see without any prejudice actually what is going on, both outwardly and inwardly, without any control or decision. This attention is action which is not something separate by itself, for life is action. You don't have to become an activist, which again is a fragmentation of life. If we are really concerned with total action, not a fragmentary one, then total action comes with total attention, which is to see actually *what is* both inwardly and outwardly. And that very seeing is the doing.

The Beginnings Of Learning, pp. 243-4

It was the total negation of everything known...

Meditation, in the still hours of early morning, with no car rattling by, was the unfolding of beauty. It was not thought exploring with its limited capacity nor the sensitivity of feeling; it was not any outward or inward substance which was expressing itself; it was not the movement of time, for the brain was still. It was total negation of everything known, not a reaction but a denial that had no cause; it was a movement in complete freedom, a movement that had no direction and dimension; in that movement there was boundless energy whose very essence was stillness. Its action was total inaction and the essence of that inaction is freedom. There was great bliss, a great ecstasy that perished at the touch of thought.

Krishnamurti's Notebook, p. 127

VI. In Daily Life

One cannot possibly learn it from anybody...

Meditation is one of the greatest arts in life—perhaps the greatest—and one cannot possibly learn it from anybody; that is the beauty of it. It has no technique and therefore no authority. When you learn about yourself, watch yourself, watch the way you walk, how you eat, what you say, the gossip, the hate, the jealousy—if you are aware of all that in yourself, without any choice. that is part of meditation.

So meditation can take place when you are sitting in a bus or walking in the woods full of light and shadows, or listening to the singing of birds, or looking at the face of your wife or child.

Freedom From The Known, p. 116

There is no other meditation but the meditation of daily life...

When you look at a tree, or the face of your neighbour or the face of your wife or husband, and if you look with that quality of mind that is completely quiet, then you will see something that can not be attained through any practice; if you practice a method, you are still living within a very small space which thought has created, as the 'me', the 'I', practicing, advancing; that space if full of conflict, full of its own achievements and failures; such a mind can never be quiet, do what it will.

Meditation is the understanding of pleasure and desire, understanding not suppressing, not intellectually verbalizing it or rationalizing it away—understanding this whole process of consciousness which is lived daily, with all its confusion, misery—that is meditation. There is no other meditation but the meditation of daily life—of how you act, how you think, how you feel—out of this understanding comes silence.

It is only in silence that love can exist. The quality of love is not born out of desire, conflict and all the rest of the ugliness and torture; it comes into being with the understanding of time, space, desire, pleasure; it is then that it is seen that love is not desire and pleasure. That innocent mind can solve all the problems and all the challenges that it meets. It is completely aware of all the problems of man—and it becomes immeasurable. To such a mind there is no time and no death; to come upon such a mind one has to end sorrow; the ending of sorrow is the beginning of wisdom.

KFA BULLETIN, 1977, # 32 p. 14

Meditation is not a separate thing from life...

We hardly ever listen to the sound of a dog's bark, or to the cry of a child or the laughter of a man as he passes by. We separate ourselves from everything, and then from this isolation look and listen to all things. It is this separation which is so destructive, for in that lies all conflict and confusion. If you listened to the sound of those bells with complete silence, you would be riding on it —or, rather, the sound would carry you across the valley and over the hill. The beauty of it is felt only when you and the sound are not separate, when you are part of it. Meditation is the ending of the separation, not by any action of will or desire, or by seeking the pleasure of things not already tasted.

Meditation is not a separate thing from life; it is the very essence of life, the very essence of daily living. To listen to those bells, to hear the laughter of that peasant as he walks by with his wife, to listen to the sound of the bell on the bicycle of the little girl as she passes by—it is the whole of life, and not just a fragment of it, that meditation opens.

The Only Revolution, p. 163

You can do it all day ...

Meditation is not something different from daily life; do not go off into the corner of a room and meditate for ten minutes, then come out of it and be a butcher—both metaphorically and actually. Meditation is one of the most serious things; you do it all day, in the office, with the family, when you say to somebody, 'I love you', when you are considering your children, when you educate them to become soldiers, to kill, to be nationalized, worshipping the flag, educating them to enter into this trap of the modern world; watching all that, realizing your part in it, all that is part of meditation. And when you so meditate you will find in it an extraordinary beauty; you will act rightly at every moment; and if you do not act rightly at a given moment it does not matter, you will pick it up again—you will not waste time in regret. Meditation is part of life, not something different from life.

Flight Of The Eagle, p. 45

Meditation is the flight from the known...

Thought can never penetrate very deeply into any problem of human relationship. Thought is superficial and old and is the outcome of the past. The past cannot enter into something that is totally new. It can explain the new, organize it, communicate it, but the 'word' is not the new. Thought is the word, the symbol, the image. Without this symbol is there thought? We have used thought to reconstruct, to change the social structure. Thought, being old, reforms that structure into a new pattern, based upon the old. And basically, thought is divisive, fragmentary, and whatever it does will be separative and contradictory. However much it may explain philosophically or religiously the new and necessary social structure, in it there will always be the seed of destruction, of war and of violence. Thought is not the way to the new. Only meditation opens the door to that which is everlastingly new. Meditation is not a trick of thought. It is the seeing of the futility of thought and the ways of the intellect. Intellect and thought are necessary in the operation of anything mechanical, but the intellect is a fragmentary perception of the whole and meditation is the seeing of the whole.

Intellect can operate only in the field of the known, and that is why life becomes a monotonous routine from which we try to escape through revolts and revolutions—merely to fall back once again into another field of the known. This change is no change at all as it is the product of thought which is always old. Meditation is the flight from the known. There is only one freedom: it is, from the known. And beauty and love lie in this freedom.

Five Conversations, p. 16

Then anger blossoms, grows, and naturally dies...

Meditation is one of the most important things in life—not how to meditate, not meditation according to a system, not the practice of meditation, but rather that which meditation is. If one can find out, very deeply, the significance, the necessity, and the importance of it for oneself, then one puts aside all systems, methods, gurus, together with all the peculiar things that are involved in the Eastern type of meditation.

It is very important to uncover for oneself what one actually is, not according to the theories and the assertions and experiences of psychologists, philosophers, and the gurus, but rather by investigating the whole nature and movement of oneself—by seeing what one actually is.

One does not seem to be able to understand how extraordinarily important it is to see what one is, actually, as though one were looking at oneself in a mirror, psychologically—thereby bringing about a transformation in the very structure of oneself. When one fundamentally, deeply, brings about such a transformation, or mutation, then that mutation affects the whole consciousness of man. This is an absolute fact, a reality. To bring about a fundamental transformation becomes very important, if one is at all serious, if one is concerned with the world as it is, with all its appalling misery, confusion, and uncertainty, with all the divisions of religions and nationalities, with their wars, with their accumulation of armaments, spending enormous sums to prepare for war, to kill people in the name of nationality and so on and so on.

To see what one actually is, it is vital that there be freedom, freedom from the whole content of one's consciousness—the content of consciousness being all the things put together by thought. Freedom from the content of one's consciousness, from one's angers and brutalities, from one's vanities and arrogance, from all the things that one is caught up in, is meditation. The very seeing of what one is, is the beginning of the transformation. Meditation implies the ending of all strife, of all conflict, inwardly and therefore outwardly. Actually, there is no inward or outward; it is like the sea—there is the ebb and flow.

In uncovering what one actually is, one asks: Is the observer, oneself, different from that which one observes—psychologically that is. I am angry, I am greedy, I am violent; is that I different from the thing observed, which is anger, greed, violence? Is one different? Obviously not. When I am angry there is no I that is angry, there is only anger. So anger is me; the observer is the observed. The division is eliminated altogether. The observer is the observed and therefore conflict ends.

Part of meditation is to eliminate totally all conflict, inwardly and therefore outwardly. To eliminate conflict, one has to understand this basic principle; the observer is not different from the observed, psychologically. When there is anger, there is no I, but a second later thought creates the I and says, "I have been angry," and brings in the idea that I should not be angry. So there is anger and then the I who should not be angry; the division brings conflict. When there is no division between the observer and the observed, and therefore only the thing that is, which is anger, then what takes place? Does anger go on? Or is there a total ending of anger? When anger occurs and there is no observer, no division, it blossoms and then ends—like a flower, it blooms, withers, and dies away. But as long as one is fighting it, as long as one is resisting it, or rationalizing it, one is giving life to it. When the observer is the observed, then anger blossoms, grows, and naturally dies—therefore there is no psychological conflict in it.

The Wholeness Of Life, pp. 141-2

One has to be a total outsider...

Meditation is not an escape from the world; it is not an isolating self-enclosing activity, but rather the comprehension of the world and its ways. The world has little to offer apart from food, clothes, and shelter, and pleasure with its great sorrows.

Meditation is wandering away from this world; one has to be a total outsider. Then the world has a meaning, and the beauty of the heavens and the earth is constant. Then love is not pleasure. From this all action begins that is not the outcome of tension, contradiction, the search for self-fulfilment, or the conceit of power.

The Only Revolution, p. 10

Love is meditation...

Love is meditation. Love is not remembrance, an image, sustained by thought as pleasure, nor the romantic image which sensuality builds; it is something that lies beyond all the senses and beyond the economic and social pressures of life. The immediate realization of this love, which has no root in yesterday, is meditation; for love is truth, and meditation is the discovery of the beauty of this truth. Thought cannot discover this, it can never be said, 'I have discovered' or 'I have captured that love which is of heaven'.

KFA BULLETIN, 1976, #30 p. 10

The first step is the last step...

The first step is the last step. The first step is the step of clear perception, and that act of clear perception is the last act. When you see danger, a serpent, that very perception is the complete action. Do you follow? Now we said the first step is the last step. The first step is to perceive, perceive what you are thinking, perceive your ambition, perceive your anxiety, your loneliness, your despair, this extraordinary sense of sorrow, perceive it, without any condemnation, justification, without wishing it to be different—just to perceive it, as it is. When you perceive it as it is, then there is a totally different kind of action taking place, and that action is the final action. Right? That is, when you perceive something as being false or as being true, that perception is the final action, which is the final step. Right? Now listen to it. I perceive the falseness of following somebody else, somebody else's instruction—Krishna, Buddha, Christ, it does not matter who it is. I see there is the perception or the truth that following somebody is utterly false. Right? Because your reason, your logic and everything points out how absurd it is to follow somebody. Now that perception is the final step, and when you have perceived, you leave it, forget it, because the next minute you have to perceive anew, which is again the final step. If you do not drop what you have learned, what you have perceived, then there is a continuity of the movement of thought; and the movement and continuity of thought is time. And when the mind is caught in the movement of time, it is in bondage.

So that is one of the major problems, whether the mind can be free of the past, the past regrets, the past pleasures, the memories, remembrances, incidents and experiences, all the things that one has built up, the past, which is also the 'me'. The 'me' is the past. Now, thought gives continuity to something which has been perceived clearly, and not being able to put it aside gives it a continuity which becomes the means of perpetuating thought.

You had a happy incident yesterday. You don't forget it, you do not drop it, you take it over with you, you think about it. The very thinking about something which is of the past gives continuity to the past. Therefore there is no ending to the past. You are following all this? But if you perceive that you had a most extraordinary, happy incident yesterday, see it, perceive it, and completely end it, do not carry it over, then there is no continuity as the past which thought has built. Therefore every step is the last step. Do you get it?

So we have to go into this question whether thought which is giving a continuity to memory as memory—and memory is the past—whether thought can ever come to an end. Because that is part of meditation. It is part of a total mutation of the brain cells themselves, because if there is a continuity of the movement of thought, it is the repetition of the old, because thought is memory, thought is the response of memory, thought is experience, thought is knowledge.

So our question is: Thought is always perpetuating itself through experience, through the constant repetition of certain memories. Knowledge is always in the past, and when you act according to knowledge, you are giving continuity to thought, but you must have knowledge to act technologically. See the difficulty? If you did not use thought, you could not go home, you could not work in an office. You must have knowledge, but also see the importance, the danger of a mind that is caught in the perpetual movement of thought, and therefore never seeing anything new. Thought is always old, thought is always conditioned, never free, because it is acting according to the past. So the question is, how can this movement of thought which at one level is absolutely necessary to function logically, sanely, healthily, how can this movement of thought come to an end, for a man to perceive something totally new, to live totally differently?

The traditional approach to this question is control it, hold it, or learn to concentrate. Right? Which again is absurd because who is the controller? Is not the controller part of the thought, part of the knowledge which says you must control? That is, you have been taught to control. So there is a way of observing thought without any control, without giving it a continuity, but observing so that it ends. You have understood my question? Because if thought continues, the mind is never quiet, and it is only when the mind is completely quiet that there is the possibility of perception. See the logic of it; that is, if my mind is chattering, comparing, judging, saying this is right, this is wrong, I am not listening to you. To listen to you, to understand what you are saying, I must give my attention, and to give one's attention completely, that attention itself is silence. Right?

One sees very clearly that silence is completely necessary, not only at the superficial level, but at the most deep level; at the very root of our being there must be complete silence. How is this to happen? It cannot possibly happen if there is any form of control because then there is conflict, because then there is the man who says, 'I must control', and there is the thing to be controlled. In that there is division, in that division there is conflict. Therefore, is it possible for the mind to be completely empty and quiet, not continuously but each second? That is the first perception, that the mind must be completely quiet; the perception, the truth of it and the seeing of the truth of it is the first and last step, and then that perception must be ended; otherwise, you carry it over. Therefore the mind must observe, must be aware choicelessly of every perception, and there must be the ending of that perception instantly, seeing and ending. You are following all this?

So the mind is not living with thought, which is the response of the past, and giving to that thought a continuity into the future which may be the next minute, the next second. And thought is the response of memory, which is the very structure of the brain cells themselves. If you have observed yourself, you will see that in the brain cells themselves is the material of memory, and that memory responds, which is thought. To bring about a total mutation in the quality of the cell itself, there must be an ending of every perception, understanding, seeing, acting and moving away from it, so that the mind is always perceiving and dying, perceiving the falsity of the truth and ending it and moving on without carrying the memory. Right?

You know all this demands tremendous perception, tremendous vitality, energy. To go into this step by step as we have been doing, not missing a thing, requires tremendous energy.

... How does a mind without following any system, without following any compulsion, without any comparison, how can a mind which has been so long conditioned, be completely empty of the past? You understand my question? To empty completely so that it sees clearly, and what it is seeing clearly end it, so that it is always renewing itself in emptiness, that is, renewing itself in innocence.

Now the word *innocence* means an innocent mind, means a mind that can never be hurt. The word *innocence* comes from a Latin word which means incapable of being hurt, and most of us are hurt, hurt with all the memories which we have accumulated round those hurts, our remorses, our longings, our loneliness. Our fears are part of this sense of being hurt. From childhood we are hurt consciously or unconsciously. How to empty all that hurt, not taking time, you understand, not saying, 'Gradually I will get rid of this hurt'? When you do that, you will never end it, you are dead by the end of it. So the question is whether the mind can empty itself completely, not only at the superficial level, but also at the very depth of its being, at its very roots. Because otherwise one lives in a prison, one lives in the prison of cause and effect in this world of change.

So you must ask this question, put this question to yourself, whether your mind can be empty of all its past and yet retain the technological knowledge, your engineering knowledge, your linguistic knowledge, the memory of all that, and yet function from a mind that is completely empty. The emptying of that mind comes about naturally, sweetly without bidding, when you understand yourself, when you understand what you are. What you are is the memory, bundle of memories, experiences, thoughts. When you understand that, look at it, observe it; and when you observe it, see in that observation that there is no duality between the observer and the observed; then when you see that, you will see that your mind can be completely empty, attentive, and in that attention you can act wholly, without any fragmentation. All that is part of meditation.

And when you understand totally the whole fragmentation of yourself—not integration—understand how this fragmentation and its contradiction arise, not how to bring it together. You cannot do that. To bring it together implies a duality—the one who is bringing it, bringing about integration and all that. Then when you really, deeply, profoundly understand about yourself, learn about yourself, then you can understand the meaning of time, the time that binds, holds, that brings sorrow.

If you have gone that far, and that means you have not gone far in the distance, far verbally, not measurably far, if you have gone that far, not in height or depth, if you have gone to that height of understanding, with that fullness, then you will find out for yourself a dimension which has no description, which has no word, which is not something to be bought through sacrifice, which is not in any book, which no guru can ever experience. He wants to teach you about it, how to reach it, therefore, when he says, 'I have experienced that and I know what that is', he has not experienced it, he does not know what it is. The man who says he knows does not know. So a mind must be free of the word, the image, the past, and that is the first step and the last step.

Krishnamurti In India 1970-71, pp. 50-3,55-7

VII. In Nature

Wander by the seashore...

What is important in meditation is the quality of the mind and the heart. It is not what you achieve, or what you say you attain, but rather the quality of a mind that is innocent and vulnerable. Through negation there is the positive state. Merely to gather or to live in experience denies the purity of meditation. Meditation is not a means to an end. It is both the means and the end. The mind can never be made innocent through experience. It is the negation of experience that brings about that positive state of innocency which cannot be cultivated by thought. Thought is never innocent. Meditation is the ending of thought, not by the meditator, for the meditator is the meditation. If there is no meditation, then you are like a blind man in a world of great beauty, light, and colour.

Wander by the seashore and let this meditative quality come upon you. If it does, don't pursue it. What you pursue will be the memory of what it was—and *what was* is the death of *what is.* Or, when you wander among the hills, let everything tell you the beauty and the pain of life, so that you awaken to your own sorrow and to the ending of it. Meditation is the root, the plant, the flower, and the fruit. It is words that divide the fruit, the flower, the plant, and the root. In this separation action does not bring about goodness: virtue is the total perception.

The Only Revolution, pp. 14-5

This openness was heaven...

It had rained heavily during the night and the day, and down the gullies the muddy stream poured into the sea, making it chocolate-brown. As you walked on the beach the waves were enormous and they were breaking with magnificent curve and force. You walked against the wind, and suddenly you felt there was nothing between you and the sky, and this openness was heaven. To be so completely open, vulnerable to the hills, to the sea and to man is the very essence of meditation. To have no resistance, to have no barriers inwardly towards anything, to be really free, completely, from all the minor urges, compulsions, and demands, with all their little conflicts and hypocrisies, is to walk in life with open arms. And that evening, walking there on that wet sand, with the seagulls around you, you felt the extraordinary sense of open freedom and the great beauty of love which was not in you or outside you but everywhere. We don't realize how important it is to be free of the nagging pleasures and their pains, so that the mind remains alone. It is only the mind that is wholly alone that is open. You felt all this suddenly, like a great wind that swept over the land and through you. There you were denuded of everything, empty and therefore utterly open. The beauty of it was not in the word or in the feeling, but seemed to be everywhere about you, inside you, over the waters and in the hills. Meditation is this.

Meditations, 1969, p. 7

The ecstasy of solitude...

The words *you* and *I* separate things. This division in this strange silence and stillness doesn't exist. And as you watched out of the window, space and time seemed to have come to an end, and the space that divides had no reality. That leaf and that eucalyptus and the blue shining water were not different from you.

Meditation is really very simple. We complicate it. We weave a web of ideas round it, what it is and what it is not. But it is none of these things. Because it is so very simple it escapes us, because our minds are so complicated, so time-worn and time-based. And this mind dictates the activity of the heart, and then the trouble begins. But meditation comes naturally, with extraordinary ease, when you walk on the sand or look out of your window or see those marvellous hills burnt by last summer's sun. Why are we such tortured human beings, with tears in our eyes and false laughter on our lips? If you could walk alone among those hills or in the woods or along the long, white, bleached sands, in that solitude you would know what meditation is. The ecstasy of solitude comes when you are not frightened to be alone, no longer belonging to the world or attached to anything. Then, like that dawn that came up this morning, it comes silently and makes a golden path in the very stillness, which was at the beginning, which is now, and which will be always there.

Meditations, 1969, p. 10

VIII. The Meditator

It is strange how the meditator persists...

The mind too was utterly still. After all, meditation is not a means to produce a result, to bring about a state which has been or which might be. If meditation is with intention, the desired result may be achieved, but then it is not meditation, it is only the fulfilment of desire. Desire is never satisfied; there is no end to desire. The understanding of desire, without trying to put a stop to it, or sustain it, is the beginning and the end of meditation. But there is something beyond this. It is strange how the meditator persists; he seeks to continue, he becomes the observer, the experiencer, a recollecting mechanism, the one who evaluates, accumulates, rejects. When meditation is of the meditator, it only strengthens the meditator, the experiencer. The stillness of the mind is the absence of the experiencer, of the observer who is aware that he is still. When the mind is still, there is the awakened state. You can be intently awake to many things; you can probe, seek, inquire, but these are the activities of desire, of will, of recognition and gain. That which is ever awake is neither desire nor the product of desire. Desire breeds the conflict of duality, and conflict is darkness.

Commentaries On Living, Series II, pp. 205-6

Meditation is not an intellectual process...

Meditation is a movement in attention. Attention is not an achievement, for it is not personal. The personal element comes in only when there is the observer as the centre, from which he concentrates or dominates; thus all achievement is fragmentary and limited. Attention has no border, no frontier to cross; attention is clarity, clear of all thought. Thought can never make for clarity, for thought has its roots in the dead past; so thinking is an action in the dark. Awareness of this is to be attentive. Awareness is not a method that leads to attention; such attention is within the field of thought and so can be controlled or modified; being aware of this inattention is attention. Meditation is not an intellectual process—which is still within the area of thought. Meditation is the freedom from thought, and a movement in the ecstasy of truth.

The Only Revolution, p. 107

Meditation has significance only when there's an understanding of the meditator

Meditation has significance only when there's an understanding of the meditator. In practising what you call meditation, the meditator is apart from the meditation, isn't he? Why is there this difference, this gap between them? Is it inevitable, or must the gap be bridged? Without really understanding the truth or the falseness of this apparent division, the results of so-called meditation are similar to those which can be brought about by any tranquillizer that is taken to quiet the mind. If one's purpose is to bring thought under domination, then any system or drug that produces the desired effect will do.

'But you wipe away at one stroke all the yogic exercises, the traditional systems of meditation that have been practised and advocated through the centuries by the many saints and ascetics. How can they all be wrong?'

Why shouldn't they all be wrong? Why this gullibility? Is not a tempered scepticism helpful in understanding this whole problem of meditation? You accept because you are eager for results, for success; you want to 'arrive'. To understand what meditation is, there must be questioning, inquiry; and mere acceptance destroys inquiry. You have to see for yourself the false as the false, and the truth in the false and the truth as the truth; for none can instruct you concerning it. Meditation is the way of life, it is part of daily existence, and the fullness and beauty of life can only be understood through meditation. Without understanding the whole complexity of life, and the everyday reactions from moment to moment, meditation becomes a process of self-hypnosis. Meditation of the heart is the understanding of daily problems. You can't go very far if you don't begin very near.

'I can understand that. One cannot climb the mountain without first going through the valley. I have endeavoured in my daily life to remove the obvious barriers, like greed, envy, and so on, and somewhat to my own surprise I have managed to put aside the things of the world. I quite see and appreciate that a right foundation must be laid; otherwise, no building can stand. But meditation isn't merely a matter of taming the burning desires and passions. The passions must be subjugated, brought under control; but surely, sir, meditation is something more than this, isn't it? I am not quoting any authority, but I do feel that meditation is something far greater than merely laying the right foundation.'

That may be; but at the very beginning is the totality. It is not that one must first lay the right foundation, and then build, or first be free from envy, and then 'arrive'. In the very beginning is the ending. There's no distance to be covered, no climbing, no point of arrival. Meditation itself is timeless; it's not a way of arriving at a timeless state. It *is*, without a beginning and without an ending. But these are mere words, and they will remain as such as long as you don't inquire into and understand for yourself the truth and the falseness of the meditator.

'Why is that so important?'

The meditator is the censor, the watcher, the maker of 'right' and 'wrong' effort. He's the centre, and from there he weaves the net of thought; but thought itself has made him; thought has brought about this gap between the thinker and the thought. Unless this division ceases, so-called meditation only strengthens the centre, the experiencer who thinks of himself as apart from the experience. The experiencer is always craving more experience; each experience strengthens the accumulation of past experiences, which in turn dictates, shapes the present experience. Thus the mind is ever conditioning itself. So experience and knowledge are not the liberating factors that they are supposed to be.

Commentaries On Living, Series III, pp. 144-5

The meditator can never know the goodness of meditation...

It had been raining recently, and the grass in the cemetery was dazzlingly green. All around it were palm and banana trees, and flowering bushes. It was a pleasant place, and children would come to play on the grass under the trees, where there were no graves. Early in the morning, long before the sun was up, there was heavy dew on the grass, and the tall palms stood out against the starlit sky. The breeze from the north was fresh, and it brought with it the long moan of a distant train. Otherwise it was very quiet; there were no lights in the surrounding houses, and the rattle of lorries on the road had not yet begun.

Meditation is the flowering of goodness; it is not the cultivation of goodness. What is cultivated never endures; it passes away, and has to be started again. Meditation is not for the meditator. The meditator knows how to meditate; he practises, controls, shapes, struggles, but this activity of the mind is not the light of meditation. Meditation is not put together by the mind; it's the total silence of the mind in which the centre of experience, of knowledge, of thought, is not. Meditation is complete attention without an object in which thought is absorbed. The meditator can never know the goodness of meditation.

Commentaries On Living, Series III, p. 274

The meditator can act only in the field of the known...

Meditation is a very important action in life; perhaps it is the action that has the greatest and deepest significance. It is a perfume that cannot easily be caught; it is not to be bought through striving and practice. A system can yield only the fruit it offers; and the system, the method, is based on envy and greed. Not to be able to meditate is not to be able to see the sunlight, the dark shadows, the sparkling waters, and the tender leaf. But how few see these things! Meditation has nothing to offer; you may not come begging with folded hands. It doesn't save you from any pain. It makes things abundantly clear and simple; but to perceive this simplicity the mind must free itself, without any cause or motive, from all the things it has gathered through cause and motive. This is the whole issue in meditation. Meditation is the purgation of the known. To pursue the known in different forms is a game of self-deception, and then the meditator is the master, there is not the simple act of meditation. The meditator can act only in the field of the known; he must cease to act for the unknown to be. The unknowable doesn't invite you, and you cannot invite it. It comes and goes as the wind, and you cannot capture it and store it away for your benefit, for your use. It has no utilitarian value, but without it life is measurelessly empty.

Commentaries On Living, Series II, p. 218

The meditator is the meditation...

Have you ever gone into this question of meditation, any of you? Meditation is not concerned with meditation but with the meditator—do you see the difference? Most of you are concerned with meditation, what to do about it, how to meditate step by step and so on—that is not the question at all. The meditator *is* the meditation. To understand the meditator is meditation.

Now if you have gone into this question of meditation, the meditator must come to an end, by understanding, not by suppressing, not by killing thought. That is, to understand oneself is to understand the movement of thought; thought being the movement of the brain with all its memories—the movement of thought seeking security, and all the rest of it.

Now the meditator is asking, can this brain become completely quiet? Which is, can thought be completely still, and yet operate out of this stillness not as an end in itself. Probably all this is too complicated for you; it's really quite simple.

Impossible Question, p. 187

There is no meditator in meditation. If there is, it is not meditation...

He always liked machinery; he dismantled the motor of a car and when it ran it was as good as new. When you are driving, meditation seems to come so naturally. You are aware of the countryside, the houses, the farmers in the field, the make of the passing car, and the blue sky through the leaves. You are not even aware that meditation is going on, this meditation that began ages ago and would go on endlessly. Time isn't a factor in meditation, nor the word which is the meditator. There's no meditator in meditation. If there is, it is not meditation. The meditator is the word, thought and time, and so subject to change, to the coming and going. It's not a flower that blooms and dies. Time is movement. You are sitting on the bank of a river, watching the waters, the current and the things floating by. When you are in the water, there's no watcher. Beauty is not in the mere expression, it's in the abandonment of the word and expression, the canvas and the book.

Krishnamurti's Journal, p. 12

It was meditation without the meditator...

It was quite early in the morning and it was still dark. The night was thunderous and rainy; windows banged and rain was pouring into the room. Not a star was visible, the sky and the hills were covered with clouds, and it was raining with fury and noise. On waking, the rain had stopped and it was still dark. Meditation is not a practice, following a system, a method; these only lead to the darkening of the mind, and it is ever a movement within the boundaries of the known; there is despair and illusion within their activity. It was very quiet so early in the morning, and not a bird or leaf was stirring. Meditation which began at unknown depths and went on with increasing intensity and sweep carved the brain into total silence, scooping out the depths of thought, uprooting feeling, emptying the brain of the known and its shadow. It was an operation and there was no operator, no surgeon; it was going on, as a surgeon operates for cancer, cutting out every tissue which has been contaminated, lest the contamination should again spread. It was going on, this meditation, for an hour by the watch. And it was meditation without the meditator. The meditator interferes with his stupidities and vanities, ambitions and greed. The meditator is thought, nurtured in these conflicts and injuries, and thought in meditation must totally cease. This is the foundation for meditation.

Krishnamurti's Notebook, pp. 158-9

Forget the word *meditation*...

It was a marvellous morning and the cool air which was becoming colder wrapped round you, and you were completely lost to everything. There was nothing and beyond nothing.

You should really forget the word *meditation*. That word has been corrupted. The ordinary meaning of that word—to ponder over, to consider, to think about—is rather trivial and ordinary. If you want to understand the nature of meditation you should really forget the word because you cannot possibly measure with words that which is not measurable, that which is beyond all measure. No words can convey it, nor any systems, modes of thought, practice or discipline. Meditation—or rather, if we could find another word which has not been so mutilated, made so ordinary, corrupt, which has become the means of earning a great deal of money—if you can put aside the word, then you begin quietly and gently to feel a movement that is not of time. Again, the word movement implies time—what is meant is a movement that has no beginning or end. A movement in the sense of a wave: wave upon wave, starting from nowhere and with no beach to crash upon. It is an endless wave. Time, however slow it is, is rather tiresome. Time means growth, evolution, to become, to achieve, to learn, to change. And time is not the way of that which lies far beyond the word *meditation*. Time has nothing to do with it. Time is the action of will, of desire, and desire cannot in any way [word or words inaudible here]—it lies far beyond the word meditation.

Here, sitting on that rock, with the blue sky—it is astonishingly blue—the air is so pure, unpolluted. Far beyond this range is the desert. You can see it, miles of it. It is really a timeless perception of that which is. It is only that perception which can say it is.

You sat there watching for what seemed many days, many years, many centuries. As the sun was going down to the sea you made your way down to the valley and everything around you was alight, that blade of grass, that sumac [a wild bush], the towering eucalyptus and the flowering earth. It took time to come down as it had taken time to go up. But that which has no time cannot be measured by words. And meditation is only a word. The roots of heaven are in deep abiding silence.

Krishnamurti to Himself, pp. 18-19

IX. Silence, Space, and the Timeless

Meditation implies a complete radical change of the mind and the heart...

We have to alter the structure of our society, its injustice, its appalling morality, the divisions it has created between man and man, the wars, the utter lack of affection and love that is destroying the world. If your meditation is only a personal matter, a thing which you personally enjoy, then it is not meditation. Meditation implies a complete radical change of the mind and the heart. This is only possible when there is this extraordinary sense of inward silence, and that alone brings about the religious mind. That mind knows what is sacred.

Beyond Violence, p. 133

This meditative mind is the religious mind...

A meditative mind is silent. It is not the silence which thought can conceive of; it is not the silence of a still evening; it is the silence when thought—with all its images, its words and perceptions—has entirely ceased. This meditative mind is the religious mind—the religion that is not touched by the church, the temples or by chants.

The religious mind is the explosion of love. It is this love that knows no separation. To it, far is near. It is not the one or the many, but rather that state of love in which all division ceases. Like beauty, it is not of the measure of words. From this silence alone the meditative mind acts.

The Only Revolution, p. 115

The meditative mind flows in this silence...

That night, particularly in that distant valley with the most ancient hills with their peculiar shaped boulders, the silence was as real as the wall you touched. And you looked out of the window at the brilliant stars. It was not a self-generated silence; it was not that the earth was quiet and the villagers were asleep, but it came from everywhere—from the distant stars, from those dark hills, and from your own mind and heart. This silence seemed to cover everything from the tiniest grain of sand in the river-bed—which only knew running water when it rained—to the tall, spreading banyan tree and a slight breeze that was now beginning. There is the silence of the mind which is never touched by any noise, by any thought or by the passing wind of experience. It is this silence that is innocent, and so endless. When there is this silence of the mind, action springs from it, and this action does not cause confusion or misery.

The meditation of a mind that is utterly silent is the benediction that man is ever seeking. In this silence every quality of silence is.

There is that strange silence that exists in a temple or in an empty church deep in the country, without the noise of tourists and worshippers; and the heavy silence that lies on water is part of that which is outside the silence of the mind.

The meditative mind contains all these varieties, changes and movements of silence. This silence of the mind is the true religious mind, and the silence of the gods is the silence of the earth. The meditative mind flows in this silence, and love is the way of this mind. In this silence there is bliss and laughter.

The Only Revolution, p. 32

There is no sequence in meditation...

There is no sequence in meditation. There is no continuity, for this implies time and space and action within that. Our whole psychological activity is within the field of time and space, and from this follows action which is always incomplete. Our mind is conditioned to the acceptance of time and space. From here to there, the chain of this and that, is time-sequence. In this movement action will bring about contradiction and therefore conflict. This is our life. Can action ever be free of time, so that there are neither regrets nor anticipation, the backward and forward looking of action? Seeing is acting. It is not first understanding and then acting, but rather seeing which in itself is action. In this there is no element of time, so the mind is always free. Time and space are the way of thought which builds and nourishes the self, the me and the not-me, with all its demands for fulfilment, its resistance and fear of being hurt.

On this morning the quality of meditation was nothingness, the total emptiness of time and space. It is a fact and not an idea or the paradox of opposing speculations. One finds this strange emptiness when the root of all problems withers away. This root is thought, the thought that divides and holds. In meditation the mind actually becomes empty of the past, though it can use the past as thought. This goes on throughout the day, and at night sleep is the emptiness of yesterday, and therefore the mind touches that which is timeless.

The Beginnings Of Learning, p. 240

Meditation breaks down the frontiers of consciousness...

Meditation breaks down the frontiers of consciousness; it breaks down the mechanism of thought and the feeling which thought arouses. Meditation caught in a method, in a system of rewards and promises, cripples and tames energy. Meditation is the freeing of energy in abundance; and control, discipline, and suppression spoil the purity of that energy. Meditation is the flame burning intensely without leaving any ashes. Words, feeling, thought, always leave ashes and to live on ashes is the way of the world. Meditation is danger for it destroys everything; nothing whatsoever is left, not even a whisper of desire, and in this vast, unfathomable emptiness there is creation and love.

Krishnamurti's Notebook, p. 110

When there is that meditative mind, it has its own ecstasy...

Questioner: What do you mean by *ecstasy*, can you describe it? You said, ecstasy is not pleasure, love is not pleasure.

Krishnamurti: What is ecstasy? When you look at a cloud, at the light in that cloud, there is beauty. Beauty is passion. To see the beauty of a cloud or the beauty of light on a tree, there must be passion, there must be intensity. In this intensity, this passion, there is no sentiment whatsoever, no feeling of like or dislike. Ecstasy is not personal; ecstasy is not yours or mine, just as love is not yours or mine. When there is pleasure it is yours or mine. When there is that meditative mind it has its own ecstasy—which is not to be described, not to be put into words.

Questioner: Are you saying that there is no good and bad, that all reactions are good—are you saying that?

Krishnamurti: No, sir, I did not say that. I said, observe your reaction, do not call it good or bad. When you call it good or bad you bring about contradiction. Have you ever looked at your wife—I am sorry to keep at it—without the image that you have about her, the image that you have put together over thirty or so years? You have an image about her and she has an image about you; these images have relationship; you and she do not have relationship. These images come into being when you are not attentive in your relationship—it is inattention that breeds images. Can you look at your wife without condemning, evaluating, saying she is right, she is wrong, just observe without bringing in your prejudices? Then you will see there is a totally different kind of action that comes from that observation.

The Flight of the Eagle, p. 106

Meditation is the emptying of consciousness of its content...

Time has bred consciousness with its content. It is the culture of time. Its content makes up consciousness; without it, consciousness, as we know it, is not. Then there is nothing. We move the little pieces in this consciousness from one area to another according to the pressure of reason and circumstance, but in the same field of pain, sorrow, and knowledge. This movement is time, the thought and the measure. It is a senseless game of hide and seek with yourself, the shadow and substance of thought, the past and the future of thought. Thought cannot hold this moment, for this moment is not of time. This moment is the ending of time; time has stopped at that moment, there is no movement at that moment, and so it is not related to another moment. It has no cause and so no beginning and no end. Consciousness cannot contain it. In that moment of nothingness, everything is.

Meditation is the emptying of consciousness of its content.

Krishnamurti's Journal, pp. 99-100

To meditate is to transcend time...

To meditate is to transcend time. Time is the distance that thought travels in its achievements. The travelling is always along the old path covered over with a new coating, new sights, but always the same road, leading nowhere except to pain and sorrow.

It is only when the mind transcends time that truth ceases to be an abstraction. Then bliss is not an idea derived from pleasure but an actuality that is not verbal.

The emptying of the mind of time is the silence of truth, and the seeing of this is the doing; so there is no division between the seeing and the doing. In the interval between seeing and doing is born conflict, misery, and confusion. That which has no time is the everlasting.

The Only Revolution, p. 145

Meditation is always new...

Meditation is always new. It has not the touch of the past for it has no continuity. The word *new* doesn't convey the quality of a freshness that has not been before. It is like the light of a candle which has been put out and relit. The new light is not the old, though the candle is the same. Meditation has a continuity only when thought colours it, shapes it, and gives it a purpose. The purpose and meaning of meditation given by thought becomes a time-binding bondage. But the meditation that is not touched by thought has its own movement, which is not of time. Time implies the old and the new as a movement from the roots of yesterday to the flowing of tomorrow. But meditation is a different flowering altogether. It is not the outcome of the experience of yesterday, and therefore it has no roots at all in time. It has a continuity which is not that of time. The word *continuity* in meditation is misleading, for that which was, yesterday, is not taking place today. The meditation of today is a new awakening, a new flowering of the beauty of goodness.

The Only Revolution, pp. 127-8

X. Otherness

You cannot possibly invite the other...

Verbally we can go only so far: what lies beyond cannot be put into words because the word is not the thing. Up to now we can describe, explain, but no words or explanations can open the door. What will open the door is daily awareness and attention—awareness of how we speak, what we say, how we walk, what we think. It is like cleaning a room and keeping it in order. Keeping the room in order is important in one sense but totally unimportant in another. There must be order in the room, but order will not open the door or the window. What will open the door is not your volition or desire. You cannot possibly invite the other. All that you can do is to keep the room in order, which is to be virtuous for itself, not for what it will bring. To be sane, rational, orderly—then perhaps, if you are lucky, the window will open and the breeze will come in. Or it may not. It depends on the state of your mind. And that state of mind can be understood only by yourself, by watching it and never trying to shape it, never taking sides, never opposing, never agreeing, never justifying, never condemning, never judging—which means watching it without any choice. And out of this choiceless awareness, perhaps the door will open, and you will know what that dimension is in which there is no conflict and no time.

Freedom From The Known, p. 33

Meditation was going on below the words and the beauty of the night...

Walking and talking, meditation was going on below the words and the beauty of the night. It was going on at a great depth, flowing outwardly and inwardly; it was exploding and expanding. One was aware of it; it was happening; one wasn't experiencing it, experiencing is limiting; it was taking place. There was no participation in it; thought could not share it for thought is such a futile and mechanical thing anyhow, nor could emotion get entangled with it; it was too disturbingly active for either. It was happening at such an unknown depth for which there was no measurement. But there was great stillness. It was quite surprising and not at all ordinary.

The dark leaves were shining and the moon had climbed quite high; she was on the westerly course and flooding the room. Dawn was many hours away and there was not a sound; even the village dogs, with their shrill yapping, were quiet. Waking, it was there, with clarity and precision; the otherness was there and waking up was necessary, not sleep; it was deliberate, to be aware of what was happening, to be aware with full consciousness of what was taking place. Asleep, it might have been a dream, a hint of the unconscious, a trick of the brain, but fully awake, this strange and unknowable otherness was a palpable reality, a fact and not an illusion, a dream. It had a quality, if such a word can be applied to it, of weightlessness and impenetrable strength. Again these words have certain significance, definite and communicable, but these words lose all their meaning when the otherness has to be conveyed in words; words are symbols but no symbol can ever convey the reality. It was there with such incorruptible strength that nothing could destroy it for it was unapproachable. You can approach something with which you are familiar; you must have the same language to commune, some kind of thought process, verbal or non-verbal; above all there must be mutual recognition. There was none. On your side you may say it is this or that, this or that quality, but at the moment of the happening there was no verbalization, for the brain was utterly still, without any movement of thought. But the otherness is without relationship to anything, and all thought and being is a cause-effect process, and so there was no understanding of it or relationship with it. It was an unapproachable flame, and you could only look at it and keep your distance. And on waking suddenly, it was there. And with it came unexpected ecstasy, an unreasonable joy; there was no cause for it for it has never been sought or pursued. There was this ecstasy on waking again at the usual hour; it was there and continued for a lengthy period of time.

Krishnamurti's Notebook, pp. 148-9

Imagination and illusion are purged from the mind...

Woke up early with that strong feeling of otherness, of another world that is beyond all thought; it was very intense and as clear and pure as the early morning cloudless sky. Imagination and illusion are purged from the mind for there is no continuance. Everything is and it has never been before. Where there is a possibility of continuance, there is delusion.

It was a clear morning, though soon clouds would be gathering. As one looked out of the window, the trees, the fields were very clear. A curious thing is happening; there is a heightening of sensitivity. Sensitivity not only to beauty but also to all other things. The blade of grass was astonishingly green; that one blade of grass contained the whole spectrum of colour; it was intense, dazzling and such a small thing, so easy to destroy. Those trees were all of life, their height and their depth; the lines of those sweeping hills and the solitary trees were the expression of all time and space; and the mountains against the pale sky were beyond all the gods of man. It was incredible to see, feel, all this by just looking out of the window. One's eyes were cleansed.

It is strange how during one or two interviews that strength, that power filled the room. It seemed to be in one's eyes and breath. It comes into being, suddenly and most unexpectedly, with a force and intensity that is quite overpowering, and at other times it's there, quietly and serenely. But it's there, whether one wants it or not. There is no possibility of getting used to it, for it has never been nor will it ever be. But it's there.

The process has been mild, these talks and seeing people probably make it so.

Krishnamurti's Notebook, pp. 38-9

As one walked along the street...

As one walked along the street of few palms, the otherness came like a wave that purified and strengthened; it was there like a perfume, a breath of immensity. There was no sentiment, the romance of illusion, or the brittleness of thought; it was there, sharp and clear, without any vague possibility, unhesitating, definite. It was there, a holy thing and nothing could touch it, nothing could break its finality. The brain was aware of the closeness of the passing buses, the wet street, and the squealing brakes; it was aware of all these things and, beyond, the sea, but the brain had no relation to any of these things; it was completely empty, without any roots, watching, observing out of this emptiness. The otherness was pressing in with sharp urgency. It was not a feeling, a sensation, but as factual as the man who was calling. It was not an emotion that changes, varies and continues, and thought could not touch it. It was there with the finality of death which no reason could dissuade. As it had no roots and relation, nothing could contaminate it; it was indestructible.

Krishnamurti's Notebook, p. 145

It was waiting there...

Of a sudden it happened, coming back to the room; it was there with an embracing welcome, so unexpected. One had come in only to go out again; we had been talking about several things, nothing too serious. It was a shock and a surprise to find this welcoming otherness in the room; it was waiting there with such open invitation that an apology seemed futile. Several times, on the Common, [Wimbledon Common. He was remembering London where he had stayed in May...] far away from here under some trees, along a path that was used by so many, it would be waiting just as the path turned; with astonishment one stood there, near those trees, completely open, vulnerable, speechless, without a movement. It was not a fancy, a self-projected delusion; the other, who happened to be there, felt it too; on several occasions it was there, with an all-embracing welcome of love, and it was quite incredible; every time, it had a new quality, a new beauty, a new austerity. And it was like that in this room, something totally new and wholly unexpected. It was beauty that made the entire mind still and the body without a movement; it made the mind, the brain, and the body intensely alert and sensitive; it made the body tremble, and in a few minutes that welcoming otherness was gone, as swiftly as it must have come.

Krishnamurti's Notebook, p. 150

For the otherness was there, and coming up the valley; it was like a curtain...

The house was a mile or so away among the green, luscious rice fields and silent. One had often seen it, as the road went on to the mouth of the valley and beyond it; it was the only road in and out of the valley by car and foot. The white house among few trees had been there for some years, and it had always been a pleasant sight, but seeing it, that evening, as the road turned, there was an altogether different beauty and feeling about it. For the otherness was there, and coming up the valley; it was like a curtain of rain but only there was no rain; it was coming as a breeze comes, soft and gently and it was there inside and outside. It was not thought, it was not feeling, nor was it a fancy, a thing of the brain. Each time it is so new and amazing, the pure strength and vastness of it, that there is astonishment and joy. It is something totally unknown and the known has no contact with it. The known must wholly die for it to be. Experience is still within the field of the known, and so it was not an experience. All experience is a state of immaturity. You can only experience and recognize as experience something which you have already known. But this was not experienceable, knowable; every form of thought must cease and every feeling; for they are all known and knowable; the brain and the totality of consciousness must be free of the known and be empty without any form of effort. It was there, inside and outside; one was walking in it and with it. The hills, the land, the earth were with it.

Krishnamurti's Notebook, p. 158

If it comes, it is there, without invitation...

It had been a very hot day and in that hot hall with a large crowd, it was suffocating. But in spite of all this and tiredness, woke up in the middle of the night with the otherness in the room. It was there with great intensity, not only filling the room and beyond but it was there deep down within the brain, so profoundly that it seemed to go through and beyond all thought, space, and time. It was incredibly strong, with such energy that it was impossible to be in bed; and on the terrace, with fresh, cool wind blowing, the intensity of it continued. It went on for nearly an hour, with great force and drive; all the morning it had been there. It is not a make-believe, it's not desire taking this form of sensation, excitement; thought has not built it up from past incidents; no imagination could formulate such otherness. Strangely every time this takes place, it's something totally new, unexpected and sudden. Thought, having tried, realizes that it cannot recall what had taken place at other times nor can it awaken the memory of what had taken place this morning. It is beyond all thought, desire, and imagination. It is too vast for thought or desire to conjure it up; it is too immense for the brain to bring it about. It's not an illusion.

The strange part of all this is that one's not even concerned about all this; if it comes, it is there, without invitation, and if it doesn't, there is an indifference. The beauty and the strength of it is not to be played with; there's no invitation or denial of it. It comes and goes, as it will.

Early this morning, somewhat before sunrise, meditation, in which every kind of effort has long ago ceased, became a silence, a silence in which there was no centre and so no periphery. It was just silence. It had no quality, no movement, neither depth nor height. It was completely still. It is this stillness that had movement expanding endlessly, and the measurement of it was not in time and space. This stillness was exploding, ever moving away. But it had no centre; if there were a centre, it would not be stillness, it would be stagnant decay; it had nothing whatsoever to do with the intricacies of the brain. The quality of the stillness which the brain can bring about is entirely different, in every way, from the stillness that was there this morning. It was a stillness that nothing could disturb, for it had no resistance; everything was in it and it was beyond everything. The early morning traffic of lorries bringing foodstuff and other things to the town in no way disturbed that stillness, nor the revolving beams of light from the high tower. It was there, without time.

Krishnamurti's Notebook, pp. 114-5

The intense energy of life is always there...

In the afternoon yesterday, it began suddenly, in a room overlooking a noisy street; the strength and the beauty of the otherness was spreading from the room outward over the traffic, past the gardens and beyond the hills. It was there, immense and impenetrable; it was there in the afternoon, and just as one was getting into bed, it was there with furious intensity, a benediction of great holiness. There is no getting used to it, for it is always different; there's something always new, a new quality, a subtle significance, a new light, something that had not been seen before. It was not a thing to be stored up, remembered, and examined, at leisure; it was there and no thought could approach for the brain was still and there was no time to experience, to store up. It was there and all thought became still.

The intense energy of life is always there, night and day. It is without friction, without direction, without choice and effort. It is there with such intensity that thought and feeing cannot capture it to mould it according to their fancies, beliefs, experiences, and demands. It is there with such abundance that nothing can diminish it. But we try to use it, to give it direction, to capture it within the mould of our existence and thereby twist it to conform to our pattern, experience, and knowledge. It is ambition, envy, greed that narrow down its energy, and so there is conflict and sorrow; the cruelty of ambition, personal or collective, distorts its intensity, causing hatred, antagonism, conflict. Every action of envy perverts this energy, causing discontent, misery, fear; with fear there is guilt and anxiety and the never ending misery of comparison and irritation. It is this perverted energy that makes the priest and the general, the politician and the thief. This boundless energy made incomplete by our desire for permanency and security is the soil in which grow barren ideas, competition, cruelty, and war; it is the cause of everlasting conflict between man and man.

When all this is put aside, with ease and without effort, then only is there that intense energy which can only exist and flower in freedom. In freedom alone, it causes no conflict and sorrow; then alone it increases and has no end. It is life that has no beginning and no end; it is creation which is love, destruction.

Energy used in one direction leads to one thing, conflict and sorrow; energy that is the expression of total life is bliss beyond measure.

Krishnamurti's Notebook, pp. 136-7

XI. A Light Unto Oneself

On waking this morning, beyond all meditation and thought and the delusions that feelings create, there was an intense bright light at the very centre of the brain and beyond the brain at the very centre of consciousness, of one's being. It was a light that had no shadow nor was it set in any dimension. It was there without movement. With that light there was present that incalculable strength and beauty beyond thought and feeling.

The process was rather acute in the afternoon.

Krishnamurti's Notebook, p. 44

Freedom is to be a light to oneself; then it is not an abstraction, a thing conjured by thought. Actual freedom is freedom from dependency, attachment, from the craving for experience. Freedom from the very structure of thought is to be a light to oneself. In this light all action takes place and thus it is never contradictory. Contradiction exists only when that law, light, is separate from action, when the actor is separate from action. The ideal, the principle, is the barren movement of thought and cannot co-exist with this light; one denies the other. This light, this law, is separate from you; where the observer is, this light, this love, is not. The structure of the observer is put together by thought, which is never new, never free. There is no 'how', no system, no practice. There is only the seeing which is the doing. You have to see, not through the eyes of another. This light, this law, is neither yours nor that of another. There is only light. This is love.

Krishnamurti's Journal, p. 29

At the bend of the road, the road gently goes down across a couple of bridges over dry red riverbeds, to the other side of the valley. The bullock cart had gone down that road; some villagers were coming up it, shy and noiseless; there were children playing in the riverbed and a bird kept on calling. Just as the road turned east, that otherness came. It came pouring down in great waves of benediction, splendid and immense. It seemed as though the heavens opened and out of this immensity came the unnameable; it had been there all day, one realized suddenly and only now, walking alone, with the others a little way off, did one realize the fact, and what made it extraordinary was this thing that was happening; it was the culmination of what had been going on and not an isolated incident. There was light, not of the setting sun nor powerful artificial light; this makes shadows but there was light without shadow and it was light.

Krishnamurti's Notebook, p. 175

It was a clear morning of winter, cold but bright, and there was not a cloud in the sky. As you watched the light of the early morning sun on the river, meditation was going on. The very light was part of that meditation when you looked at the bright dancing water in the quiet morning—not with a mind that was translating it into some meaning, but with eyes that saw the light and nothing else.

Light, like sound, is an extraordinary thing. There is the light that painters try to put on a canvas; there is the light that cameras capture; there is the light of a single lamp in a dark night, or the light that is on the face of another, the light that lies behind the eyes. The light that the eyes see is not the light on the water; that light is so different, so vast that it cannot enter into the narrow field of the eye. That light, like sound, moved endlessly—outward and inward—like the tide of the sea. And if you kept very still, you went with it, not in imagination or sensuously; you went with it unknowingly, without the measure of time.

The beauty of that light, like love, is not to be touched, not to be put into a word. But there it was—in the shade, in the open, in the house, on the window across the way, and in the laughter of those children. Without that light what you see is of so little importance, for the light is everything; and the light of meditation was on the water. It would be there in the evening again, during the night, and when the sun rose over the trees, making the river golden. Meditation is that light in the mind which lights the way for action: and without that light there is no love.

The Only Revolution, pp. 68-69

XII. The Ground

Listening in the darkness...

K: How am I to dispel this continuous, constant darkness? That is the only question, because, as long as that exists, I create this constant division. You see, this is going round in circles. I can only dispel the darkness through insight, and I cannot have that insight by any effort of will, so I am left with nothing. So what is my problem? My problem is to perceive the darkness, to perceive the thought that is creating darkness, and to see that the self is the source of this darkness. Why can't I see that? Why can't I see it, even logically?

DB: Well, it's clear logically.

K: Yes, but somehow it doesn't seem to operate. So what shall I do? I realize for the first time that the self is creating the darkness which is constantly breeding division. I see that very clearly.

DB: And the division produces the darkness anyway.

K: Vice versa, back and forth. And from all that, everything begins. I see that very clearly. What shall I do? So I don't admit division.

Q: Krishnaji, aren't we introducing division again, never the less, when we say there is the man who needs insight?

K: But man has insight. 'X' has insight, and he has explained very clearly how darkness has vanished. I listen to him, and he says your very darkness is creating the division. Actually, there is no division, no division as light and darkness. So he asks me, can you banish, can you put away this sense of division?

DB: You seem to be bringing back a division by saying that, by saying that I should do it, you see.

K: No, not 'should'.

DB: In a way you are saying that the thought process of the mind seems spontaneously to produce division. You say, try to put it aside, and at the same time it is trying to make division.

K: I understand. But can my mind put away division? Or is that a wrong question?

Q: Can it put away division as long as it is divided?

K: No, it can't. So what am I to do?

Listen. 'X' says something so extraordinarily true, of such immense significance and beauty that my whole being says, 'Capture it'. That is not a division.

I recognize that I am the creator of division, because I am living in darkness, and so out of that darkness I create. But I have listened to 'X', who says there is no division. And I recognize that is an extraordinary statement. So the very saying of that to one who has lived in constant division has an immediate effect. Right?

DB: I think that one has to, as you say, put away the division...

K: I will leave that; I won't put it away. That statement that there is no division—I want to get at that a little bit. I am getting somewhere with it.

'X's' statement from this insight, that there is no division, has a tremendous effect on me. I have lived constantly in division, and he comes along and says there is no division. What effect has it on me?

DB: Then you say there is no division. That makes sense. But on the other hand it seems that the division exists.

K: I recognize the division, but the statement that there is no division has this immense impact on me. That seems natural, doesn't it? When I see something that is immovable, it must have some effect on me. I respond to it with a tremendous shock.

DB: You see, if you were talking about something which was in front of us, and you said, 'No, it is not that way', then that would, of course, change your whole way of seeing it. Now you say this division is not that way. We try to look and see if that is so—right?

K: I don't even say, 'Is that so?' 'X' has very carefully explained the whole business, and he says at the end of it that there is no division. And I am sensitive, watching very carefully, and realizing that I am constantly living in division. When 'X' makes that statement it has broken the pattern.

I don't know if you follow what I am trying to explain? It has broken the pattern, because he has said something which is so fundamentally true. There is no God and man. Right, Sir, I stick to that. I see something—which is, where hatred exists the other is not. But, hating, I want the other. So constant division is born out of darkness. And the darkness is constant. But I have been listening very carefully, and 'X' makes a statement which seems absolutely true. That enters into me, and the act of his statement dispels the darkness. I am not making an effort to get rid of darkness, but 'X' is the light. That's right, I hold to that.

So it comes to something, which is, can I listen with my darkness—in my darkness, which is constant? In that darkness, can I listen to you? Of course I can. I am living in constant division which brings darkness. 'X' comes along and tells me there is no division.

DB: Right. Now why do you say you can listen in the darkness?

K: Oh, yes, I can listen in darkness. If I can't I am doomed.

DB: But that is no argument.

K: Of course that is no argument, but it is so!

DB: Living in darkness is not worthwhile. But now we say that it is possible to listen in the darkness.

K: He, 'X', explains to me very, very carefully. I am sensitive, I have been listening to him in my darkness, but that is making me sensitive, alive, watching. That is what I have been doing. We have been doing it together. And he makes a statement that there is absolutely no division. And I know that I am living in division. That very statement has brought the constant movement to an end.

Otherwise, if this doesn't take place I have nothing—you follow? I am perpetually living in darkness. But there is a voice in the wilderness, and listening to that voice has an extraordinary effect.

DB: Listening reaches the source of the movement, whereas observation does not.

K: Yes, I have observed, I have listened, I have played all kinds of games all my life. And I now see that there is only one thing. That there is this constant darkness and I am acting in the darkness—in this wilderness which is darkness, whose centre is the self. I see that absolutely, completely; I can't argue against it any more. And 'X' comes along and tells me this. In that wilderness a voice says there is water. You follow? It is not hope. There is immediate action in me.

One must realize that this constant movement in darkness is my life. You follow what I am saying? Can I, with all the experience, with all the knowledge which I have gathered over a million years, suddenly realize that I am living in total darkness? Because that means I have reached the end of all hope. Right? But my hope is also darkness. The future is out altogether, so I am left with this enormous darkness, and I am there. That means, the realization of that is the ending of becoming. I have reached that point and 'X' tells me this is natural.

You see, all the religions have said this division exists.

DB: But, they say it can be overcome.

K: It is the same pattern repeated. It doesn't matter who said it, but the fact is somebody in this wilderness is saying something, and in that wilderness I have been listening to every voice, and to my own voice, which has created more and more darkness. Yet, this is right. That means, doesn't it, that when there is insight there is no division?

DB: Yes.

K: It is not your insight or my insight, it is insight. In that there is no division.

DB: Yes.

K: Which brings us to that ground we spoke of...

DB: What about the ground?

K: In that ground there is no darkness as darkness, or light as light. In that ground, there is no division. Nothing is born of will, or time, or thought.

DB: Are you saying that light and darkness are not divided?

K: Right.

DB: Which means to say there is neither.

K: Neither, that's it! There is something else. There is a perception that there is a different movement, which is 'non-dualistic'.

DB: Non-dualistic means what? No division.

K: No division. I won't use 'non-dualistic'. There is no division.

DB: But nevertheless there is movement.

K: Of course.

DB: What does that mean now, without division?

K: I mean by movement, that movement which is not time. That movement doesn't breed division. So I want to go back, lead to the ground. If, in that ground, there is neither darkness nor light, no God or the son of God—there is no division—what takes place? Would you say that the ground is movement?

DB: Well, it could be, yes. Movement is undivided.

K: No. I say there is movement in darkness.

DB: Yes, but we said there is no division of darkness and light, and yet you said there is movement.

K: Yes. Would you say the ground is endless movement?

DB: Yes.

K: What does that mean?

DB: Well, it is difficult to express.

K: Keep on going into it; let's express it. What is movement, apart from movement from here to there, apart from time—is there any other movement?

DB: Yes.

K: There is. The movement from being to becoming, psychologically. There is the movement of distance, there is the movement of time. We say those are all divisions. Is there a movement which in itself has no division? When you have made that statement that there is no division, there is that movement surely?

DB: Well, are you saying that when there is no division that movement is there?

K: Yes, and I said, 'X' says that is the ground.

DB: Right.

K: Would you say it has no end, no beginning?

DB: Yes.

K: Which means again time.

DB: Can one say that movement has no form?

K: No form—all that. I want to go a little further. What I am asking is, we said that when you have stated there is no division, this means no division in movement.

DB: It flows without division, you see.

K: Yes, it is a movement in which there is no division. Do I capture the significance of that? Do I understand the depth of that statement? A movement in which there is no division, which means no time, no distance as we know it. No element of time in it at all. So I am trying to see if that movement is surrounding man?

DB: Yes, enveloping.

K: I want to get at this. I am concerned with mankind, humanity, which is me. 'X' has made several statements, and I have captured a statement which seems so absolutely true—that there is no division. Which means that there is no action which is divisive.

DB: Yes.

K: I see that. And I also ask, is that movement without time, etc? It seems that it is the world, you follow?

DB: The universe.

K: The universe, the cosmos, the whole.

DB: The totality.

K: Totality. Isn't there a statement in the Jewish world, 'Only God can say "I am"'?

DB: Well, that's the way the language is built. It is not necessary to state it.

K: No, I understand. You follow what I am trying to get at?

DB: Yes, that only this movement *is*.

K: Can the mind be of that movement? Because that is timeless, therefore deathless.

DB: Yes, the movement is without death; in so far as the mind takes part in that, it is the same.

K: You understand what I am saying?

DB: Yes. But what dies when the individual dies?

K: That has no meaning, because once I have understood there is no division...

DB: ...then it is not important.

K: Death has no meaning.

DB: It still has a meaning in some other context.

K: Oh, the ending of the body: that's totally trivial. But you understand? I want to capture the significance of the statement that there is no division, it has broken the spell of my darkness, and I see that there is a movement, and that's all. Which means death has very little meaning.

DB: Yes.

K: You have abolished totally the fear of death.

DB: Yes, I understand that when the mind is partaking in that movement, then the mind is that movement.

K: That's all! The mind is that movement.

The Ending of Time, pp. 144-51
Conversation with Prof. David Bohm

XIII. Short Quotations

Meditation is a process of awareness in action.

Ojai, 7th Public Talk, 1940

Thought is mechanical and meditation is not.

The Beginnings Of Learning, p. 250

Meditation is the movement of love.

Meditations, 1969, p. 5

Meditation of the heart is the understanding of daily problems.

Commentaries On Living, Series III, p. 144

Meditation itself is timeless; it's not a way of arriving at a timeless state.

Commentaries On Living, Series III, p. 145

To understand the meditator is meditation.

Impossible Question, p. 187

Where there is control, there is no meditation of the heart.

Adyar, 4th Public Talk, 1934

Only meditation opens the door to that which is everlastingly new.

Five Conversations, p. 16

Meditation is the ending of the word. Silence is not induced by a word, the word being *thought*. The action out of silence is entirely different from the action born of the word; meditation is the freeing of the mind of all symbols, images, and remembrances.

The Only Revolution, pp. 120-121

BIBLIOGRAPHY

The Awakening of Intelligence, Harper & Row, 1973

Beginnings of Learning, Harper & Row, 1975

Beyond Violence, Harper & Row, 1973

The Collected Works of J. Krishnamurti, Kendall/Hunt, 1991-92
Vol I (1933-34) *The Art of Listening*
Vol II (1934-35) *What Is Right Action?*
Vol III (1936-44) *The Mirror of Relationship*
Vol IV (1945-48) *The Observer Is the Observed*
Vol V (1948-49) *Choiceless Awareness*
Vol VI (1949-52) *The Origin of Conflict*
Vol VII (1952-53) *Tradition and Creativity*
Vol VIII (1953-55) *What Are You Seeking?*
Vol IX (1955-56) *The Answer Is in the Problem*
Vol X (1956-57) *A Light to Yourself*
Vol XI (1958-60) *Crisis in Consciousness*
Vol XII (1961) *There Is No Thinker, Only Thought*
Vol XIII (1962-63) *A Psychological Revolution*
Vol XIV (1963-64) *The New Mind*
Vol XV (1964-65) *The Dignity of Living*
Vol XVI (1965-66) *The Beauty of Death*
Vol XVII (1966-67) *Perennial Questions*

Commentaries on Living, First Series,
The Theosophical Publishing House, 1956

Commentaries on Living, Second Series,
The Theosophical Publishing House, 1958

Commentaries on Living, Third Series,
The Theosophical Publishing House, 1960

The Ending of Time, Harper & Row, 1985

The First and Last Freedom, Harper & Row, 1975

Five Conversations, Krishnamurti Foundation Trust, Ltd., 1970

The Flame of Attention, Harper & Row, 1983

The Flight of the Eagle, Harper & Row, 1971

Freedom From the Known, Harper & Row, 1969

The Impossible Question, Harper & Row, 1972

KFA BULLETIN #4, Krishnamurti Foundation of America, 1969

KFA BULLETIN #14, Krishnamurti Foundation of America, 1972

KFA BULLETIN #30, Krishnamurti Foundation of America, 1976

KFA BULLETIN #32, Krishnamurti Foundation of America, 1977

Krishnamurti on Education, Harper & Row, 1974

Krishnamurti to Himself, Harper & Row, 1987

Krishnamurti in India, Krishnamurti Foundation of India, 1971

Krishnamurti's Journal, Harper & Row, 1982

Krishnamurti's Notebook, Harper & Row, 1976

Meditations, 1969, Krishnamurti Foundation Trust, Ltd.

Meditations, Harper & Row, 1979

The Network of Thought, Harper & Row, 1982

The Only Revolution , Harper & Row, 1970

Think on These Things, San Francisco: Harper & Row, 1989

The Wholeness of Life, Harper & Row, 1979

You Are the World, Harper & Row, 1972

THE COLLECTED WORKS OF J. KRISHNAMURTI

(18 Volumes)

ISBN : 978-81-208-3090-5 (Set)

Rs. 350 (each volume)

The Art of Listening	Volume 1	(1933-1934)
What is Right Action?	Volume 2	(1934-1935)
The Mirror of Relationship	Volume 3	(1936-1944)
The Observer Is the Observed	Volume 4	(1945-1948)
Choiceless Awareness	Volume 5	(1948-1949)
The Origin of Conflict	Volume 6	(1949-1952)
Tradition and Creativity	Volume 7	(1952-1953)
What Are You Seeking?	Volume 8	(1953-1955)
The Answer Is in the Problem	Volume 9	(1955-1956)
A Light to Yourself	Volume 10	(1956-1957)
Crisis in Consciousness	Volume 11	(1958-1960)
There Is No Thinker, Only Thought	Volume 12	(1961)
A Psychological Revolution	Volume 13	(1962-1963)
The New Mind	Volume 14	(1963-1964)
The Dignity of Living	Volume 15	(1964-1965)
The Beauty of Death	Volume 16	(1965-1966)
Perennial Questions	Volume 17	(1966-1967)
The Concordance Index	Volume 18	(Index for Vols 1-17)

Published by :

MOTILAL BANARSIDASS PUBLISHERS PRIVATE LIMITED • DELHI

For further information about Krishnamurti Libraries, Retreats, Study Centers, Schools and events worldwide, as well as other publications, please contact the following:

Krishnamurti Foundation of America
P.O. Box 1560
Ojai, California 93024 U.S.A.
E-mail: kfa@kfa.org
www.kfa.org

Krishnamurti Foundation Trust, Ltd.
Brockwood Park
Bramdean, Hampshire
England SO24 0LQ
E-mail: info@brockwood.org.uk
www.brockwood.org.uk

Krishnamurti Foundation India
64-65 Greenways Road
Vasanta Vihar
Chennai
India 600 028
E-mail: kfihq@vsnl.com
www.kfionline.org

Also visit the website
jkrishnamurti.org